Non-Profit Booster

10 STEPS TO BUILDING A SUCCESSFUL ORGANISATION

Bybreen Samuels

Insights to Impact
London, England

NON-PROFIT BOOSTER

Bybreen Samuels

**Insights
to Impact**

Published by: Insights to Impact Publishing
London, England.

feelinggood@nonprofitbooster.com
www.nonprofitbooster.com

ISBN Regular Print Edition: 97809928832-0-1
The moral right of Bybreen Samuels to be identified as
the author of this work has been asserted in accord-
ance with the Copyright, Designs and Patents Act of
1988.

Printed and bound in the UK by Berforts Information
Press.

A CIP record for this book is available from the British
Library.

What others are saying about this book

"A refreshing guide purposefully designed to keep organisations on the right track and upgrade their outlook. And it will be valuable to all stakeholders from the governing body through to the part time ICT assistant."

Kristine Wellington, Organisational Manager, Hackney Council for Voluntary Services

"Running a charity is a complex business. Non Profit Booster provides very useful and succinct insights that will help organisations with this challenging, but rewarding task."

Judith Moran, CEO, Quaker Social Action

"If you are striving for a perfect service, because you care about getting the basics right, like delivering unexpected value and building emotional engagement with those you serve, then Non Profit Booster, is a great companion for your journey."

Steve Maingot, Chair, Southside Partnership

Disclaimer

This book is designed to provide information about the subject matter covered. It is sold with the understanding that the publisher and author are not engaged in rendering legal, accounting or other professional services. If legal or other expert assistance is required, the services of a competent professional should be sought.

It is not the purpose of this book to reprint all the information that is otherwise available to non-profit organisations, but to complement, amplify and supplement other texts.

Every effort has been made to make this book as complete and as accurate as possible. This text should only be used as a general guide and not as the ultimate source for developing non-profit organisations. Furthermore, this book contains information only up to the printing date.

The purpose of this book is to educate. The author and publisher shall have neither liability nor responsibility to any person or entity with respect to any loss or damage caused or alleged to be caused directly or indirectly by the information contained in this book.

Contents

Acknowledgements

Thanks so much to all these wonderful people who joined me on my journey to bring Non-Profit Booster to life. I value all contributions from; Kristine Wellington, Alexis Keir, Andy Gregg, Edie Fassnidge, Samantha Mauger Goretti Considine, Tesse Akpeki, Steve Maingot, Karen Mercer, Cemanthe McKenzie, Tim Carr, Eithne Rynne, Yen Nyeya, Ashley Whittley, Ade Adetosoye, Judith Moran, Jan Knight, Lana Hersak, Marina Cantacuzino, Ian Redding, Caroline Criado-Perez, Phillip Davis and Bob Thust. Their experiences and understanding of developing non-profit charitable organisations and sharing examples of good practice and expectations from the private and public sectors, are gratefully received.

Thanks also to Jane Roberts and Salvatore Circelli, for taking the time to proofread the manuscripts. And many thanks to Lisa Langley for using her editorial expertise to polish the book's content.

Also, I give additional praise to some of the mavericks, sages and leaders that really inspire me, but who I don't know personally:

Ricardo Semler, Oprah Winfrey, Barack Obama, Lilou Mace, Wayne Dyer, Louise Hay, Gary Vaynerchuk, Maya Angelou, Richard Branson, Alan Sugar, Michelle Obama, Chris Gardner and Daisaku Ikeda.

"It is not the strongest of species that survive. Nor the most intelligent but the one that is most responsive to change."

Charles Darwin

Introduction

When was the last time that your organisation was recognised for successfully delivering results for your beneficiaries and other stakeholders? Last month? Last year? Or, before the recession started in 2008?

Over the last few years, charities, voluntary and community organisations have been seriously affected by public sector cuts to grant funding. This has resulted in organisations closing down, merging with others, reducing service delivery or trying to find ways to remain relevant to stakeholders and becoming financially self-sustaining.

If any of this resonates with you, then congratulations for picking up this book. It's clear that you are action-orientated and want to bring about changes that can help to develop your organisation.

This book is not a policy thesis on the non-profit sector. Nor is it a historical tome charting the development of the sector. Rather, it offers strategies, suggestions and tactics on how organisations can improve their operations to become more effective in the 21st century. The style of the book is easy reference, concise and practical.

The guidance in this book can apply to all organisations. However, the primary audience is small and developing organisations generating an annual turnover anywhere from a micro income through to £1 million pounds.

I was inspired to write this book after I delivered a training seminar to a range of small charitable organisations that are passionate about meeting the needs of local people in their communities. During the seminar one person asked a question about strategy which led to a varied and detailed discussion.

Throughout this I was met with a chorus of, "Bybreen, what about....?" Or "Bybreen, can I quickly ask you this...." Or, "I didn't know that." Although a lot of the participants have been involved with their organisations for a long time, the nature of their questions indicated there were fundamental issues and skills they were unaware of and were lacking.

Furthermore, their questions and concerns were not unfamiliar. I have encountered them in one form or another from a multitude of organisations, since I started working in the charity sector, from the 1990s.

I want to offer practical insights to these organisations. They often do not have easy access to a combination of tactical and contemporary business skills that can be used to navigate a path towards effectiveness and sustainability. I used these skills successfully when I raised £895,775, in one application, for a charity part-nership in London.

My own experience of working with organisations has shown me several things. On the one hand there is a continued dedication to wanting to improve the lives of service users. However, this can be compromised due to not having enough paid staff to manage increasing workloads.

Conversely, passion and conviction to a mission statement needs to be bolstered by savvy, entrepre-neurial approaches that are being incorporated by all sectors, to navigate a new way forward. More often than not, small organisations do not have the capacity to keep abreast of external developments and practices to build their infrastructure and brand identity leading to improved brand awareness.

Non-Profit Booster is my way of sharing what I have learnt and how you may use it to enhance your organisation. So if you are ready, let's begin!

[1]

Leadership...Oh yes we can should and must!

Before you even think about raising money to deliver services to your beneficiaries, you must establish a firm internal foundation for your organisation. Essentially, how you do this is conveyed by the statutory responsibility in the Charities Acts 1992, 1993, 2006 and 2011. They clearly define the range of expectations, roles and responsibilities.

And these are implemented by the two sets of leaders within your organisation. Firstly, trustees or otherwise referred to as the management committee, or board of directors, undertake the legal role of governance. And the chief executive officer, director or co-ordinator leads the day to day operations. A summary of the practical roles and responsibilities of trustees are to:

- ➢ Define the organisation's vision, mission and values. Essentially, know what you're aiming for, work out how it will be done and understand what you want to be recognised and known for when others connect with your brand.

- ➢ Provide strategic development in relation to positioning the organisation in the external environment and creating a plan to help you get there.

- ➢ Establish systems, programmes, services and products that the organisation is going to deliver. These should flow from the vision that you've cultivated and as a response to your beneficiaries.

- ➢ Design an income generation strategy and actively participate in activities to cultivate resources.

- ➢ Create a financial investment template that helps to set and monitor budgets and spending. Also, identify prudent investment options that will enable assets to grow and be protected.

- ➢ Demonstrate your ability to be a good employer by having transparent recruitment, selection, induction and training processes and opportunities for staff. Provide direct support to the director while he or she performs their role.

➢ Lead and enhance the organisation's brand. Become known as the organisation's strategic advocates.

➢ Recruit new trustees and induct them into their roles. Give clear directions about what is expected of them. Understand what their strengths and weaknesses are and find ways to utilise their strengths.

➢ Operate a democratic style board and method of conducting meetings. Find ways to be inclusive, productive and effective. Periodically, undertake board assessments to ascertain current levels of efficiency regarding board responsibility.

Governance expert, Tesse Akpeki of Tesse Akpeki Associates offers trustees this **practical tip,** to increase their understanding of their roles.

"Go to an induction meeting and spend time in the organisation to actually see the work that is being done. Attend briefing sessions before going to board meetings so that you can participate more effectively in them.

Integrate the organisation's services into board meetings by including governance or mission statement moments, during discussions. This will help trustees to better appreciate the service outcomes."

In addition, there are three activities that you can do to enhance the experience of trustees that can be easily implemented:

1. Identify what inspired them to join your board. Find out if they have expectations that have yet to be realised. If this is the case, explore ways in which the organisation can satisfy them. If it transpires that this is not the case, discuss how their wishes can be readjusted.

2. Undertake an analysis of your board and high-light the gaps in areas of expertise. Follow this up with a survey of the skills and knowledge of trustees and the networks they are connected to.

3. Highlight organisations that are known for demonstrating good practice and areas of excellence. Liaise with them about mentoring opportunities to your board of trustees. In addition, co-opt people onto your board to help bolster its effectiveness.

Enlightened leadership

Leadership styles are changing and becoming more sharply defined in the 21st century. Authoritarian and hierarchical approaches are being rapidly replaced by collaboration and inclusion. Employees expect a greater level of effectiveness from their leaders, irrespective of the sector they represent.

A leader who I find truly inspirational and has practiced enlightened leadership, since the 1980s, is Ricardo Semler. He is the Chairman and Owner of the Semco Group of Companies, based in Brazil. Furthermore, he is the author of two bestselling books, Maverick and The Seven Day Weekend. Semler took a visionary approach to employee relationships. For example:

- Staff hire and fire their own managers.
- Staff decide their own salaries.
- Staff decide their own hours of work.
- There are no rule books.

He developed an ideology of corporate democracy. This includes treating his staff as intelligent adults who want to live self-determined lives both at work and at home.

Leaders from companies, institutions and non-profit organisations travel from across the world to see Semco in action. They want to see how this workplace nirvana operates in real life. Semler recognises that his concepts and practices are unusual and challenging to the conventional way of employee engagement. But they work.

A 2010 report by Kenexa Research Institute revealed the five factors employees use to rate the effectiveness of their leaders. They are:

1. The ability to convey a clear message.
2. The ability to handle business challenges.
3. A commitment to delivering high quality services and products.
4. The demonstrable ability to value employees.
5. Having the confidence of employees.

Gaining the confidence of employees also involves the ability to mobilise and motivate others to achieve goals. The attributes leaders need to do this are having an approachable character, honesty, courage and the ability to relate and communicate to a wide range of people. By demonstrating these traits leaders will act like a magnet to those seeking a responsive leader. In the current climate of running organisations where instability exists, people seek security from leaders they can believe in because of who they are and the values they stand for.

> **Excerpt of a Leadership Case Study Ade Adetosoye, Former Divisional Director of Social Care, London Borough of Lambeth**
>
> "When I took over the Children and Young People's Service it was under a 'special measures' assessment by Ofsted. I worked with my colleagues to transform the Service which led the Division to be later assessed as 'outstanding' by Ofsted. I spent time:
>
> ➤ Working with colleagues to help them regain their self-belief and aiding them to see how they add value to children and families.
>
> ➤ Setting up a learning and development section and created an Aspiring Managers Programme which trained senor social workers into management positions.
>
> ➤ Setting up forums so that all staff could give me direct feedback.
>
> ➤ Holding monthly meetings with de-motivated staff to find solutions.
>
> As a leader, it's important to me to listen to my staff, respond to their concerns and take care of them. If I don't take care of them, then how can I expect them to take care of our service users?"

Managers and leaders

There are some distinguishing features between these two roles. Four general distinctions between them are that managers' strengths tend to include:

1. Being tactical by translating the annual strategy into manageable units that can be understood by others, so that they are able to execute.

2. Being motivational in how they enable their staff to achieve their goals efficiently and effectively.

3. Delivering the message from the leadership team that continually highlights what needs to be achieved and how it will be done.

4. Being transactional by keeping abreast of activities through supervision, monitoring and team meetings.

Conversely, leaders lean towards:

➢ Being a visionary, creating a picture of what the future looks like for the organisation and then designing the structural blueprint.

➢ Taking an inspirational approach that evokes a positive and action-orientated behaviour in others.

➢ Persuasively communicates the direction of the organisation and engages others to follow on the journey.

➢ Being transformational by re-imagining the organisation's future and leading everyone to realising it.

Kristine Wellington, Organisational Development Manager at Hackney Council for Voluntary Services, offers this **practical tip** about other considerations for leaders.

"Trustees and leaders have to maintain a balance between developing the organisation and delivering the service. Too often there is more focus on delivery than influencing social change and reshaping policy. At times this could be due to a lack of confidence in terms of taking their daily service delivery evidence to decision makers, to advocate for better services for their users. Funders could support this aspect by providing funding for skills' development. This is separate from funding for service delivery."

What is the difference between an organisational strategy and tactics?

Every organisation should have a strategy because it states the long-term objectives, development and evolution of the organisation's vision. This lays out what it ultimately wants to achieve for its beneficiaries. To help the definition of the strategy, leaders need to gather information:

> ➢ About the external environment and opportunities for growth.

> ➢ Understand and promote the internal strengths.

> ➤ Provide solutions to reverse weaknesses.

In addition, they need to know the core competencies of the organisation and access additional skills and resources to bring the strategy to life. Lastly, they have to communicate the strategy to all relevant people, in a way that they will be able to understand and implement.

Conversely, tactics are the essential stepping stones that are necessary to bring the strategy to life. They are the bricks and mortar for your organisation's strategic building that on a yearly, incremental basis achieves the overall outcomes. Tactics are formulated once the strategy has been clearly defined.

Given that the strategy is the starting point, to ensure its successful implementation, trustees must discuss and allocate responsibilities to everyone in the organisation. Success is achieved when your whole team understands how your brand, service or product is received by your beneficiaries and stakeholders.

As the leadership team, you must find ways to demonstrate the purpose and values of the organisation at all times. This will help everyone to absorb the message and present a unified front when engaging with the public. If you leave this role to chance, people will give varied interpretations which in turn will dilute your brand and will undermine your strategy.

In order for the strategy to materialise you have to communicate what the vision of the organisation will look like by the end of a specific period of time. This should be followed up by allocating actions to colleagues to bring about the desired outcomes.

Organisational culture

A way in which you can ascertain your organisation's culture is to try and define its personality. Give consideration to how the organisation generally responds to stimuli that touches it. For example:

> ➢ How receptive are the trustees and the director to suggestions about improving communications?

> ➢ How does the organisation praise and reward staff for doing great work?

> ➢ Do contentious organisational issues get swept under the carpet?

In terms of relating to the culture, you are trying to identify and understand the organisation's habits that have developed over the course of its existence. Factors that can help you to explore these are; identifying key historical events, any traditions that have been created, knowing the circumstances and people who created them, the types of myths or stories that exist about the organisation and understanding the leadership and management styles.

Excerpt of a Culture Case Study – Judith Moran, CEO, Quaker Social Action

"During the early stages of the recession and public sector funding cuts, the trustees and I reviewed all of the budgets. We had to find ways to reduce costs or consider redundancies. We asked staff to take a pay cut. We gave them all the information, i.e. current finances, reserves, rationale and the savings we could make.

The union consulted with everyone. One of the things that really warmed my heart was that when the staff team were asked anonymously whether they would prefer redundancy or take a pay cut, everyone said they would rather take a pay cut than see one of their colleagues lose their job. We tapered the cuts along a sliding scale from 0 – 5%.

I took 5% and those on lower salaries remained unaffected. Everyone pulled together to continue delivering the service. Halfway through the year when our financial situation improved we reimbursed everyone the amount of salary they had lost to date. Our staff were amazed and astonished and their trust in me and the board has risen even further."

Other elements that can help you create a strong positive culture are:

> ➤ Organisational values shared by trustees, staff and volunteers.

> ➢ A unified and clear approach in terms of relating to the external environment and stake-holders.

> ➢ A set of rituals and procedures that everyone should follow.

> ➢ Informal networks that aid communication.

> ➢ Organisational heroes and heroines who repre-sent the organisation and communicate its values.

We have an opportunity to deliver our services internationally, how do we begin to prepare for this?

Giving consideration to the following areas will help to improve your strategy:

> ➢ If there are language differences think about who could help you bridge this gap. Search for local collaborators or partners to help you achieve your goals.

> ➢ Gather information on social norms, culture, laws and national attitudes. All sectors operate in a global market and there is a growing expectation for strategists to demonstrate some awareness of these areas.

- ➤ Look for insights about the behaviours of your competitors.

- ➤ Keep abreast of political events in terms of signs that strengthen your intentions.

- ➤ Look for any signs of instability that could undermine your plans.

- ➤ Create both formal and informal occasions to exchange ideas and information with people in your network who can help to strengthen your strategy.

- ➤ Think through how your service or product will be delivered or distributed, both on and offline. Compare this to how it is usually accessed in the country you are hoping to enter.

- ➤ Weigh up the risk factors and explore if there are any barriers to entry.

- ➤ Give consideration to how you will overcome any barriers.

Yen Nyeya, CEO of GHARGWEG offers this **practical tip.**

"Organisations must be sustainable in their own country before considering service delivery abroad. Think through whether you have enough staff to deliver the service and whether you do or not, consider working with partners. Conduct a due diligence process for example, we frequently travel to Ghana and have met a range of people and organisations. We review their funding streams and see if they've received any public awards.

Furthermore, we are keen to know the quality of their work and if they are involved in any partnerships. This background knowledge helps to inform our decisions."

Digital ability

In addition to the growing expectation for cultural fluency, leaders should also know how to flex their digital muscles. This is in relation to grasping the importance of utilising their online networks effectively. The reason for this is that where a good rapport exists with followers, leaders can ask them to help solve problems, source information, pilot new ideas or proposals, wield influence in their sector or niche market, make referrals and recruit new staff.

As online, virtual worlds continue to increase and hold our attention leaders can start to build their reputation by producing interesting and valuable content that will appeal to their followers. They may be motivated to circulate the content to friends and colleagues in their networks. This in turn will strengthen the leader's reputation.

Another way for leaders to enhance their reputation is to demonstrate their expertise by connecting with other experts in their field and exchanging information that enables growth and development. Furthermore, if there is a way for a leader to position themselves as a connector between disparate groups of people, this will also help to increase their influence. Examples of digital tools that can assist in assessing the strength of your online reputation are: Klout, Identified and Peer Index. Your online inter-actions will be scored on the basis of the number of people you influence, the extent to which this happens and the people in your network.

Leadership...Oh yes we can, should and must!

Mini workout

1. Describe the compelling vision that trustees have for your organisation.

2. Name the top 3 competencies of your organisation.

3. Who is the most memorable past Chair and CEO? What behaviours or activities are still associated with them?

4. What is the most striking attribute about the current Board of Trustees and CEO? How can you build upon it?

5. Identify a key event that happened in the organisation. What emotional effect does it still have?

[2]

Business model
Does one size fit all?

With the diminishing public purse, organisations are now very much in the position where they have to think differently in terms of raising money to deliver services. A business model is a process that helps to explain how income is going to be generated. It is fundamentally aligned to knowing and understanding your defined audiences. The business model answers whether the organisation is satisfying a need, solving a problem or a combination of both. Further, it includes a comprehensive structure that grounds the customer's experience and expectations, both internally and externally.

Business models differ from business plans in that a business plan is a set of intentions over a specific period of time of what the organisation plans to do. This is highlighted by laying out its strategic objectives, the business environment, competitive analysis and financial projections. A business plan is a static document.

Conversely, the business model is tactical, flexible and allows for monitoring and evaluating the implementation of the model on a regular basis. The business model is always working towards satisfying the value proposition.

The value proposition helps an organisation to tightly focus on its customers' experience by detailing what it will actually do for them. To answer this, the key question that trustees and staff should ask is, 'how are we creating value by satisfying a customer need or solving a problem?

'

Rationale for your work

A useful approach to understand why you do what you do is to imagine yourself as a beneficiary. The meaning for your product and service derives from a situation in their world that needs a solution. This will help to reconcile their situation in some way as a result of receiving your input. To explore the perspectives of your beneficiaries think through these questions:

> ➢ What type of aspirations do our beneficiaries have? How can we help to fulfil them?

> ➤ What type of problems do they encounter in their everyday lives? How can we eradicate them?

> ➤ What is really important to them that they feel is beyond their reach? What prevents them from achieving this?

Some organisations mistakenly lean towards relying on secondary research to build their operations and activities. Your first port of call must be your beneficiaries because you exist primarily to deliver services and products directly to them. Therefore, as your primary audience, you can communicate directly with them to find out what their needs and problems are. Regular contact with your audience helps to sharpen your practices, approaches and your offerings. Beyond face to face dialogue, social media tools such as Facebook, blogs, Pinterest and Twitter can help to facilitate discussion. They are easy, accessible and create immediacy. You can also use the online resource, www.surveymonkey.com to create questionnaires to gather responses.

Secondary research can be used to substantiate the information gained from your beneficiaries. Bear in mind that this type of research, like government reports are written as one way dialogue that was generated during a fixed period of time.

Examine the external environment

The environment can be explored both strategically and tactically. Key considerations are:

➤ Knowing the factors that impact upon the macro market you are operating in.

➤ Gauging the lifespan of the sector or market.

➤ Finding evidence that could indicate if the sector or market will be short, medium or long term.

➤ Following political developments that could support or undermine your organisation's strategy and objectives.

➤ Understanding the laws that could affect your organisation.

➤ Noting societal changes that have an impact on the demographics of your target audience.

➤ Having an awareness of factors that could affect staff, volunteers and board members.

➤ Awareness of any barriers that could prevent your organisation from entering or expanding into a particular sector or market.

Growth opportunities

A route into uncovering opportunities is to concentrate on the opportunities segment of your S.W.O.T. analysis.

When exploring this section think about:

> Your target audience – have their needs changed? Or do you see future changes on the horizon?

> Other organisations and individuals who you could collaborate with or develop joint venture relationships.

> Emerging and current political, economic and social developments.

> The benefits of new technology and how they could pave the way to strengthening your growth.

> The effectiveness of your social media strategy.

> How a change in government or legislation can provide a time for growth.

> How you can provide solutions to the unexpressed needs of your target audience.

Innovation

Asking, 'what if' type of questions, are an easy way to start exploring innovative approaches to service delivery. These questions allow you to suspend your belief about the limits on what type of products and services can be created and delivered. The type of team players that you need on board to open up this process should be diverse in age, experience, stakeholder knowledge of beneficiaries, professional expertise, race and culture. This rich mix of perspectives will aid the discovery of multiple possibilities that could bring about an enriching organisational experience.

When the team has been assembled, choose the area for innovation then undertake research in areas such as beneficiary behaviour, new technologies and practices from other sectors, markets and competitors. Generate as many ideas as possible and define criteria to reduce the ideas into a list of a few that you can give deeper consideration to. When prioritising your innovations, you could assess them in terms of:

➢ How long it will take to implement the change?

➢ How much will it cost?

➢ What type of response could we expect from our beneficiaries and relevant stakeholders?

Revenue streams

Depending on the type of service or product offering, here are typical revenue streams that can generate income for your organisation:

- Sell assets such as books, research reports, CDs and DVDs.
- Licence training programmes and materials.
- Hire fees for exhibition materials.
- Charge subscription fees if customers want to gain continuous access to a particular service, such as using the internet and computer equipment.
- Sell your service solutions to the statutory sector to assist them to meet their objectives.

"A significant shift in mindset is required by trustees. For instance, if services are commissioned then the money received is earned income, not grant aid. Purchasers should be treated as clients instead of funders. The business model should reflect service characteristics, accountability, leadership, personalisation and innovation that is responsive to changes in the environment." **Steve Maingot, Chair, Southside Partnership**

Barriers to designing and implementing a new business model

Five obstacles that prevent change are:

> A fearful organisational culture that is also risk averse.

> Successes can blind leaders to consider other ways to enhance the organisation.

> Not keeping abreast of environmental and market developments.

> Lack of a common framework, language and practice to discuss business model development and innovation.

> Lack of organisational vision, poor governance and leadership. This could be due to trustees being unsure of what to do because they lack tactical and technical knowledge and are part of a 'rubber stamp' committee, where the board relies solely on the judgement and decision of the Chair. Alternatively, the committee dynamics are full of conflict therefore it is difficult for decisions to be made.

Samantha Mauger, CEO of Age UK London offers this **practical tip.**

"Too many organisations have closed down because they didn't diversify their income streams and were over-reliant on local authority funding. An income portfolio can include; statutory funding, earned income, local community income and trust funding. Involve your beneficiaries in the design, monitoring and evaluation of services because you will always be in a position to deliver tailored services to meet their specific needs. As a result of this clarity, organisations have a stronger basis upon which to generate more income."

Business model evaluation

An effective way to approach your evaluation is to compartmentalise each aspect of your business model and then apply a SWOT assessment to it. The strengths and weaknesses relate to your internal environment and the opportunities and threats refer to the external world.

Through the application of this process you want to gain insights regarding what needs to be improved to bring about a fulfilling beneficiary experience. So for example, if you want to examine your customer experience section, you could grade the experience from 1-5 when assessing the following areas:

Great customer relationship	Poor customer relationship
We always gain new customers	Rarely gain new customers
We have many customer niches	Unsure of our customer niches

Conversely, if you want to review the opportunities and threats within the value proposition segment you could answer the following:

> What other customer needs could we satisfy?

> Do we need to automate some of our relationships?

> Could we generate recurring income streams by converting services into products or vice versa?

In terms of threats you could ask questions around your infrastructure namely:

> What would happen if our partners collaborated with our competitors?

> Are any of our key activities in danger of being disrupted because of other providers?

Ashley Whittley, Development Manager, Unltd offers this **practical tip.**

"Once you've designed it, your business model should be something your neighbour can easily understand, i.e. what you're going to do, how it will be financed and resourced. If you're aiming for sustainability then you must concentrate on generating a regular income. Fundraising doesn't guarantee this and it is time intensive. Concentrate on activities or services that can generate a profit."

Business model..Does one size fit all?

Mini workout

1. How would you define your business model?

2. Name 3 secondary research reports that could support the needs of your beneficiaries.

3. Identify trends that are shaping the micro niche or market that you are delivering products and services in.

4. What are the top 3 organisational assets that could be licensed to other agencies and sectors?

5. If you have internal organisational barriers that impact on effective decision making, how can you overcome them?

[3]

Partnerships...When 2, 3, or more become 1

There is some truth in the saying, 'No man is an island.' Every day we interact with others to assist in realising personal and collective goals, dreams and desires. Organisational islands have two internal elements and at least one other external relationship that are crucial to delivering great services and establishing brand identity.

Satisfying the vision and mission of the organisation requires commitment, communication and collaboration. This can relate to a whole range of stakeholders. However, the three relationships that I want to focus on are those between the Chair and CEO, the high performance team and external organisations.

Chair and CEO – Tired or inspired partnership?

Everyone performs some type of leadership function in your organisation but the Chair and CEO hold the figurehead positions. A characteristic that is essential to their relationship as in others is, trust. Laws and legal agreements cannot legislate for human behaviour. So it is crucial that these two people spend time understanding each other and exploring ways in which a natural degree of respect and trust is built over time.

The Chair and CEO are the primary faces of your rganisation and ideally they must be unified in their methods of communicating the effectiveness of the organisation to colleagues and external stakeholders. However, the unity can be fractured or destroyed because of diminishing trust, uncertainty or suspicions about each other's motives, smouldering conflicts and intense feelings of disregard or disrespect.

As you can see from these behavioural traits it is not a weak strategy that affects the Chair / CEO partnership. It has more to do with their abilities to maintain healthy interactions that sustain trust and respect. Beyond agreement over the delivery of the vision and mission it will be useful to take time to explore who they are as people. What I mean by this is that you may want to find out the following:

> ➤ What makes him / her tick in terms of emotionally, philosophically, politically, socially and culturally?

> ➤ Is he / she a risk taker or risk averse?

> ➤ Does he / she plan things methodically, whereas you're a blue sky thinker?

> ➤ How does this person make decisions and resolve conflict in comparison to you?

Having an understanding of the makeup of your leadership partner will help to create a more rounded picture of who they are and what they stand for. If you can demonstrate your awareness of this in practical ways then you are on the road to creating a trusting relationship. With an appreciation of who each other is, you can begin to explore openly how the partnership will have to work in order to satisfy the organisation's vision and outcomes. To help communication to flow more freely give consideration to the following:

> ➤ Identify up to 10 major decisions that are central to your relationship and the organisation over the next twelve months.

> ➤ Design a decision making plan, include the level of consultation required before a decision is reached.

> ➤ Create a conflict resolution framework and system.

> ➤ Find ways to use any differences to create change that is greater than what currently exists.

As **Mahatma Gandhi** said, "Be the change you want to see."

High performance team

Great teams don't exist in isolation. They are developed in organisations that have a healthy culture. The effective demonstration of the Chair and CEO partnership will inspire board members, staff, volunteers and it will enhance the culture. The culture will already embody a very clear vision, mission, values that everyone relates to including; respecting and appreciating all personnel. This context enables people to flourish because the recognition of diverse backgrounds, experience and expertise which all help to enhance the synergy of a high-performance team.

Another feature of these teams is friendship amongst team members. This aspect increases the level of appreciation for all contributions that are made to secure the organisation's outcomes. You need a strong, dynamic team to turn your organisation's dream into a reality. So what are the key attributes of a great team player? During the recruitment process you want to identify people who demonstrate the following:

> ➤ Have a 'positive, can do' attitude.

➤ Show a desire to ensure the organisation's goals are achieved.

➤ Have an ability to support team members to express their views to lead initiatives.

➤ Are capable of taking personal responsibility for all their actions.

➤ Are able to accept and respond positively to the team guidelines and change.

➤ Have a unique skill, talent or ability.

"Team members should accept all forms of diversity and have the ability to work with, engage and enjoy the experience of working with their colleagues. Support within a functioning team environment carries us through difficult times." **Alexis Keir, CEO, Elfrida Rathbone**

Inspiring de-motivated team members

There may be times when your organisation doesn't reflect having a harmonious team. The various reasons as to why this is the case include; boredom, loss of interest, personal issues, over-reliance on the leader to always come up with solutions to everyday challenges, not utilising their natural strengths, performing tasks that do not take full advantage of their skill set.

As the leader it is your role to identify everyone's strengths and to help them build upon them. Staff should be encouraged to use their capabilities to achieve the organisation's mission.

To assist you in this situation you may want to use the essential leadership skill for the 21st century, which is coaching. A coaching process helps to bridge the gap between information and action and action and results. It's an empowering tool that can help your colleagues own the change they want to make that will help your beneficiaries to flourish.

I just want to demystify a few things about coaching. Firstly, it is not about telling people what to do. Secondly, a coach doesn't solve anyone's problem. And thirdly, coaches only ask questions and help people find their answers. Coaching exists in the spaces between information, questions and problem solving.

> "Coaching is the craft of engaging an individual in pursuit of getting good at something by providing personalised support and challenge to seek the best in themselves in service of humanity flourishing. Tagline – Coaches help you play your game better." **Dave Buck, CEO, Coachville**

Imagine this example. Darren is a CEO of a charity and due to funding cuts a number of staff have been made redundant. Staff morale is terrible and Darren has received criticism from some trustees and other colleagues about his leadership style and approach. During meetings he doesn't speak up if a controversial issue is being discussed. Also, in relation to his team if they don't know how to do something, his usual response is, 'don't worry I'll do it for you.' Darren was performing half of everyone's role which is why he was constantly overwhelmed. He's in despair and decides to have some independent coaching sessions. During the process he learnt to:

> - Identify the game that people want to play in work and life.

> - Examine the dynamics within his team.

> - Highlight the skills that people need to be successful.

> - Look for strengths and qualities that his staff want to expand on.

> - Understand what the doubts and fears are in the minds of his team.

> - Know the conflict between wanting to do great things in life and the human imperative to survive by living in a safe and controlled way.

Now with a better understanding of team esteem and dynamics Darren now handles his interactions by encouraging his staff to undertake empowered action. For example, if someone comes into his office instead of taking on or over their work Darren now asks these types of questions; what game do you want to play today? What challenges are you facing? And how is this challenge making your game more fun?

These types of questions help to invoke the spirit of play, creativity and resourcefulness. By taking actions, finding solutions and sharing, acknowledging and celebrating successes are sure ways to increase team morale and inspiration.

Coaching is an investment in staff engagement and the return on the time spent engaging is enormous. Because when leaders spend time coaching their team they perform at a higher level. As a result the leader gains back more time and staff members feel empowered, trusted and reassured. This leads to a win – win resolution for everyone.

How can we improve communication amongst the team?

To enable enhanced team performance aim to develop effective communication methods. The basis of good communication is energy, engagement and exploration. Face to face discussions are direct ways to experience whether energy is high or low. For example, if one person provides updated information in a team meeting to others, this could be limited to one directional communication. The listeners are in a passive, receptive state.

Conversely, if a team member announces a discovery or improvement this can lead to excitement, increased energy and several people talking at the same time. This shows that people are fully engaged and energy levels are spread across the team.

The third element is about exploration. This means connecting with other departments, individuals and organisations to enable fresh perspectives to be gathered. This will in turn improve the team's strategy and implementation.

In terms of priority, communicate face to face, followed by video conferencing, i.e. via Skype Google Hangouts and telephone. Lastly, use email and text, although these two are more efficient in terms of time, they are more impersonal.

A connected team helps to create further accountability to each other. And the collaborative efforts of all team members lead to achieving the desired strategic outcomes. Each person's contribution is a cog in the wheel. Therefore, they are responsible for delivering on their targets. Hold regular group meetings to discuss and measure targets against actual activity.

If there's a shortfall this creates a chance for that person to receive feedback, coaching and room for growth. It also shows where the problem areas are and how they can be rectified.

Consequently, over a period of time you may see patterns emerging, therefore monitor progress and resolve any problems. If accountability is not part of your implementation process, it becomes difficult to measure progress.

Team checklist

A checklist will teach all team members how to treat each other during difficult and easy times. Furthermore, it will help you focus on delivering your service or product that brings about the highest customer satisfaction. The standard should cover areas such as; communication, integrity, professionalism and team efficiencies. Examples of these are to:

> ➢ Speak encouragingly and with purpose.

> ➢ Take personal responsibility.

> ➢ Focus on actions and activities that work.

> ➢ Have a no blame culture.

> ➢ Create a learning, sharing and knowledge based environment.

External delivery relationships

Wide scale collaboration with other organisations to deliver services has been in vogue in the non-profit sector since Tony Blair uttered the words, 'joined-up thinking, problems and solutions.' Essentially the idea here is to strengthen the quality and range of services to local people to prevent their experiences being handled and resolved in a disjointed way before collaborative services can be delivered.

Ethine Rynne, CEO, London Voluntary Services Council, offers this **practical tip.**

"A critical question that organisations must ask themselves and their beneficiaries, during their strategic development process is, 'are we fit for purpose?' Because difficult decisions have to be made particularly as the competition for funding continues to grow during this economic climate. Currently, if a service is ineffective but there is still a need for it, then merging or partnering with other organisations, could be the solution. Also, it is a viable way to create sustainability. Governing bodies must be very clear about what they can offer a partnership."

Money tends to be the magnet that draws people to the partnership table. However, in my experience what I have not heard being clearly articulated during partnership discussions is the rationale for what brings different sectors to the table. And what I mean by this is that is all parties understand and appreciate what motivates the different sectors to come together.

For example, charities, voluntary and community organisations and social enterprises come to the partnership table because ultimately, they want to deliver enhanced or a variety of services to their beneficiaries. The rationale for the private sector to sit at the table is two-fold. Firstly, it's about improving their 'business bottom line.' Meaning, how will the partnership improve their profits? Then in addition to this, it's for altruistic reasons that help improve the lives of local communities. And lastly, the statutory sector participates in partnerships because of the additional monies received from Central Government that enables them to enhance the lives of their local constituents.

There may be an urgency to deliver solutions to your beneficiaries, but not understanding these different perspectives can create problems further down the line.

How do we create a valuable partnership?

When setting up a partnership here are some key elements to incorporate:

> ➤ All partners must understand why they want to join together to deliver services.

> Everyone should know exactly what value each partner brings to the relationship. For example, this could be expertise, innovation, contacts or a diverse perspective.

> There must be clear processes in place that show how decisions will be made and how the partnership will function.

> Partners must be willing to learn from each other. This will help to build openness and trust. Consider ways in which the partnership can establish mentoring opportunities.

> All partners must sign up and embrace a set of guiding principles.

The benefits of forming partnerships are that they provide a comprehensive way to tackle issues faced by your beneficiaries through a collaborative approach. Also, funding trends and other operational resources are targeted towards partnerships.

Partnerships embrace a variety of perspectives and as a result they have a better chance to influence decision makers who impact on the lives of your beneficiaries. Also, collaborative working helps to prevent duplication of solutions for your niche audience. In terms of developing partnerships with the business sector, **Bob Thust, Director for Responsible Business and Director for Corporate Branding at Deloitte's** offers this **practical tip.**

"Charities should consider collaborating with businesses if there is a strong connection between their mission statement and the objectives of the business. Avoid offering volunteer opportunities thinking this could be a useful strategy to gain further support from a business. Also, don't create a project from nothing, thinking this will be useful to a business.

Instead, look at each other's priorities, then explore how you could jointly create something that is mutually beneficial. Money and practical support are important But the aim of a strategic partnership is to create a legacy that continues beyond the length of the contractual arrangement. Lastly, find ways to develop relationships with other people in the business that are outside of the corporate social responsibility department."

Partnership barriers

Five reasons why organisations may not get involved in partnerships are due to:

> ➢ A lack of expertise and skills to manage a bureaucratic process.

> ➢ Partnerships can be influenced by funders' expectations. Consequently, partners have limited control.

> ➢ Resistance from some statutory partners to share power with voluntary and community partners.'

> Organisations containing people from diverse backgrounds are often poorly represented in decision-making positions in statutory sector agencies.

> The use of jargon and the formal culture of meetings may exclude people for whom English is not their first language.

Consequently, spend time going to statutory sector meetings to gain an understanding of the language, dialogue and how decisions are made. Review and implement your monitoring and evaluation processes to satisfy funder expectations. Gain confidence by valuing what contribution you bring to the partnership table. Liaise with your colleagues who have more experience with partnership dynamics to provide a glossary and explanations of language used at meetings.

One of our trustees has been asked to join an existing partnership, how can we assess if the partnership is operating to a high standard?

The types of questions you should ask to help you make a decision are:

> What are the vision, mission and strategy of the partnership?

> Do all the partners understand the purpose of the partnership?

➤ Has the partnership identified a niche target audience?

➤ Is there a realistic plan to generate revenue or raise funds from a variety of sources?

➤ Is there a clear method for recording and proving the effectiveness of the partnership on all levels?

If you receive satisfactory answers to these questions and the trustee joins the partnership then you want to be reassured that the partnership maintains a high standard. The partnership should periodically undertake the following, review:

➤ The interests and involvement of all partners. Beyond providing solutions to the beneficiaries, partners may have other interests and aspirations. Check to see if they have been met and / or whether the partnership is in a position to satisfy them.

➤ The effectiveness of the training programmes. Do they have all the necessary resources that are needed to implement them?

➤ The operational procedures that show that the partnership functions correctly. And the performance of the partnership in terms of meeting the strategic and service intentions.

Partnership...When 2, 3, 4 or more become 1

Mini workout

1. Identify 3 differences that exist between the Chair and CEO.

2. How can these differences be reconciled to create something better for the organisation?

3. Find out what are the top 2 skills each staff member possesses. And think of ways in which these skills can be integrated into the organisation.

4. Name 3 partnerships that you would like to create or join that could extend your service. What contribution can you give to the partnership?

5. What type of mentoring opportunities do you need to help you participate more effectively in partnership meetings?

[4]

Goodbye mass market
Hello savvy consumer

We are living through a time when consumer power is on the rise. Brands can no longer automatically assume loyalty from their consumers. People are making far more informed choices about the services, products, campaigns and personalities, they support. Nowadays, buy in and participation are based on individual nuanced views and perceptions. People are looking for authentic experiences and becoming more involved in the product or service design and implementation processes to ensure they get what they truly want.

"The companies that are lasting are those that are authentic. If people believe they share values with a company, they will stay loyal to the brand." **Howard Schultz, Founder and CEO, Starbucks**

The differences between old and new consumers according to **David Lewis and Darren Bridger, authors of, The Soul of the New Consumer** are as follows:

Old Consumers	New Consumers
Seek convenience	Seek authenticity
Synchronised	Individual
Less often involved	Involved
Conformist	Independent
Less well informed	Well informed

If you have a strong customer care culture then you're equipped to cater for the expectations of this new savvy consumer. If on the other hand there are obvious weaknesses, then it's time for change.

Initial steps to improve your customer care culture

Undertake a strategic review with board members, staff and volunteers. Your aim is to obtain a shared commitment to develop practices that will enhance customer engagement that leads to a fulfilling experience for them. Your operational practices should lead you directly to developing individual relationships with your customers. They should be left with a feeling that you actually care about them.

Previously, if they were dissatisfied, they would disappear from sight or share their disgruntled views with a few people. However, there are now multiple social platforms available to them to air their views on your products, services, items of interest and concerns.

An easy online tactic to use to strengthen your connection with them is to set up an organisational Twitter account. Use it to build up brand awareness with potential customers and enhancing brand identity with existing customers. Start conversations, add comments, respond to questions and suggestions, offers, advice and solutions. Also, follow blog links displayed in tweets and post meaningful responses.

Setting the tone for a customer-focused organisation

Your internal environment should be one that encourages employee happiness and wellbeing. If employees feel valued and looked after they will naturally transfer this behaviour onto service users and other stakeholders who connect with the organisation.

Trustees and the chief executive can build a positive environment by; showing open demonstrations of respect, rewarding achievements, treating staff as responsible adults who have the remit to lead the implementation of their work. This allows them to demonstrate their expertise. In addition, discuss their individual needs and if they are reasonable, find ways to fulfil them. Also, as leaders of the organisation demonstrate by example your level of self awareness about the areas of change that need to happen.

Your actions will be a great signal to staff about how to bring about the cultural change. They'll be looking to see how care, concern, sympathy and empathy can be shown to customers. Revisit your marketing budget and examine how some of the resources can be allocated towards closer customer engagement. Consult all staff as there may be hidden expertise and knowledge that could prove to be very useful. For example, staff members may also have an awareness and understanding of other organisations and companies who are blazing a trail in this area.

Furthermore, your employees are also your online and offline marketers and sales team. As a result of this they should be encouraged and empowered to blog, tweet, add Facebook comments, upload online videos on YouTube and Vimeo and post pictures on Pinterest. And lastly, respond to queries, concerns and perspectives. This level of visibility will act as a magnet to attract a wide range of stakeholders.

Lana Hersak, Development Manager at London Rebuilding Society offers this **practical tip** about creating customer focused organisation.

Fulfil the needs of your clients by involving them in designing your service or product. For example when I develop
aspects of the Mutual Aid Fund I hold focus groups with our
users to explore what they think and whether it will work.
And if not, why not? These interactions help to build loyalty
and trust."

As you develop and implement the cultural shift in the
organisation design and display a customer manifesto
in the office. This will help to motivate everyone to
bring about the best customer experience by
understanding how customers help improve the
organisation.

Customer manifesto
Benefits of good customer liaison

1. Assist you to continually create valuable services
    and products.

2. Highlight how you can cater for their needs in a
    meaningful way.

3. Help you to take a service orientated approach.

4. Guide you towards being a people centred organi-
    sation.

5. Suggest ways in which you can diversify your
    message into different languages, formats, online
    and traditional media.

6. Promote community needs and help to position your services, projects and products, in the marketplace

7. Support you to understand their emotional needs.

Who are organisational stakeholders?

They are individuals, companies, groups, institutions and sectors who have an interest in your mission statement, activities and your brand. Examples include; board members, staff, volunteers service users, customers, clients, other non-profit organisations, delivery partners, suppliers, public sector agencies, central and local government, tax inspectors, businesses, regulators and media outlets.

What is the difference between demographics and psychographics?

Gaining demographic and psychographic information about your target audience will give you a much better understanding of who they are. This will help to facilitate the creation and delivery of your services, products and programmes.

Demographics deal with external features such as age, ethnicity, race, occupation, salary, religion, marital status, hobbies and political affiliations. Alternatively, psychographics deal with desires, drives, motivations, values, expressed and unexpressed needs and wants of the people you wish to serve. Essentially, it's about why your audience buys what it buys. Becoming aware of and responding to these preoccupations will help to effectively communicate with the new consumers who want to connect with you.

What type of return on investment can we gain from engaging with our users and customers?

Deepening your relationship with stakeholders can lead them to become advocates for your brand. A central reason for this is because of the trust that has developed over time. Your advocates are more likely to be committed to your organisation and would be less inclined to buy from or engage with one of your competitors. If you sell products and services, they are more likely to increase the amount of money they spend with you. This creates a greater lifetime value to you.

And lastly, they become viral marketers because they willingly share the benefits of their engagement with you. This can be by word of mouth or by writing online reviews. The accumulation of your efforts can lead to increased brand awareness and improved customer feedback.

How can we create a buzz around our customer engagement campaign?

You can start by crafting an engaging story about your organisation. This could be shown on a community, local or regional television station. Continue discussing on Facebook and Twitter, post short videos of the story on YouTube, answering questions and responding to comments. Followers can blog or tweet about this. As a result of this type of activity your brand awareness is raised through traditional and social media working in tandem.

In addition your buzz can be created subliminally through every encounter your beneficiaries and other stakeholders have with your organisation. You can reinforce your positive image by how you make people feel through your; telephone manner, efficient response to email and query letters, face to face conversations, flowers in the reception area and printing your information on good quality paper. These types of examples can help to enhance the view others have of your organisation.

Bringing offline audiences online to continue engagement

In your marketing brochure, advertorial, radio interview or any other form of public communication, you may have included a free offer which is time limited. It may contain a link to your Facebook fan page, inviting them to click on the 'like' button to receive a voucher to access your offer. In exchange for the voucher and free gift they'll give you some background information about themselves. In the future you can continue building up your relationship with them, finding out more about their needs. This allows you to tailor solutions and services to fulfil those needs.

What type of customer relationships can we create?

Here are four examples:

> ➤ Customer collaborations in the form of working together to co-create value for all customers and the wider public. This could be free, 'how to guides' to help improve the quality of life for others.

> ➤ Community interactions between stakeholders on an online forum. They can post queries, questions, suggestions and solutions to support each other. Also if you want to pilot a new service or product, forum members can give you feedback which can help to improve your offering. And you'll gain a better understanding of their expectations.

> ➤ Customer automated service relationships are designed to give users autonomy over how they interact with your service or product. Computerised processes include personalised

and updated information that relates to their customer transactions.

➢ Tailored personal assistance where a staff member is dedicated to handling the specific needs of each customer. This relationship helps forge deeper levels of understanding, trust and changing needs, over a long period of time.

Excerpt of a case study on innovative customer care

A London based Secondary School Head Teacher shared the following in terms of her school's approach to customer care.

"It's important to create situations where you can get feedback formally, informally and anecdotally. Our first intake of pupils were unable to visit us for their Taster Day, prior to starting in the following academic year because the school building was still incomplete.

We did not want to deny them the opportunity. So, I wrote to all the parents and asked whether we could visit them at home. They agreed and between me and the deputy head, we met 180 families, over a 6 week period. We spent 45 minutes with each family. This act generated an incredible level of trust and rapport.

Parents and pupils can see and feel our school's caring ethos. So if something goes wrong at school, parents are not going to come in from the position that the school doesn't understand. They are coming from the position of, 'we know the head teacher and we trust her'. This provides a strong basis on which we can begin to discuss and resolve problems."

Goodbye mass market...Hello savvy consumer

Mini workout

1. Who are your top 3 stakeholders?

2. For each stakeholder group, design a profile that includes demographic and psychographic information.

3. What actions can you take to improve the relationship with your customers?

4. What type of time bound, useful free offer could you give to potential beneficiaries, to connect with your organisation?

5. Name 3 things that you can do to encourage employee happiness and wellbeing.

[5]

Social media...On your way to becoming online moguls

O ver the last ten years we have experienced a seismic and cultural shift in terms of how we connect and engage with each other. And the reason this has happened is because of the array of extremely effective online communication tools called Social Media.

Traditional media still has relevance in spreading your message. Sophisticated publicity campaigns and large advertising budgets are becoming a thing of the past. Both of these methods have been superseded by the nimble ability of social media. It is designed to enable you to engage directly with your beneficiaries and stakeholders in real time. There isn't a procedural time delay that impedes on your message going out and the ability for your network to respond immediately, if they so wish.

So the adage, 'small is beautiful' really works in your favour as a non-profit organisation with limited income. This is because with creative thought, time and sweat equity you can out manoeuvre larger organisations and companies. The reason for this is invariably they may have to navigate through various layers of bureaucracy and decision making, before they can agree and take their message to the world, in an authentic way.

How can we create an effective online brand?

To connect with users, customers, clients and other interested parties in today's market requires an emphasis on personal and organisational branding. Your branding will be shaped and owned by your stakeholders. Consumers look for individuals and organisations they can trust. To survive online you need to be authentic, transparent and trustworthy.

Beyond these three attributes your brand needs:

> ➤ A comprehensive organisational description that includes how consumers will benefit. You can gain recognition through your logo, relevant and frequent content, the type of media you use to market your content, i.e. video blogging, webinars and podcasts.

> ➤ Higher levels of interaction with people in your networks. Ask questions, respond to their

needs, leave comments on other people's forums and blogs and co-create content.

➢ Easy distribution of your message and content. Don't make it difficult for people to access your information. If you do you'll miss out on the golden, viral marketing opportunity that's available in social media and social networks.

➢ Locations – market your organisation through on and offline directories, Google Buzz, Twellow.com, LinkedIn, Facebook and Twitter.

➢ Exposure via your mobile phone camera and video. Create and publish content while you're active in delivering your service.

➢ Develop consistency in all your interactions.

➢ The human touch - keep talking and exploring with others to form closer ties. Find out where you may share common interests. Develop rapport and behave in a way whereby clients, customers and users really feel heard and understood.

➢ Personalised leadership that is engaging both online and offline. It's important to be visible and demonstrating what your brand stands for. This approach will help to create differentiation in the marketplace.

**Excerpt of a case study on the impact of social media–
Karen Mercer, Founder of My Coffee Stop**

"My Coffee Stop is a small business that has built a very connected community around it by doing both online and offline activities. When we launched in 2009 we set up a website, Facebook and Twitter accounts to build a presence.

As a coffee shop, the business lends itself naturally to building a community. The shop is based on a train station platform. It has a notice board and commuters who have travelled together without saying a word are now having deep conversations and making great connections. We've deepened our relationships by using social media to invite people to specific events such as our; Ideas Station Social Media Workshop, Book Club, Story Time and Sew Chatty.

Also, we use Facebook Groups to support and give advice for the community. We ask for help with social media, business and technology. It's not just us giving the answers it relies on the knowledge of the community. It feels good to see people helping each other on a forum we created and we don't have to have much input.

We have used social media to start a UK wide offline campaign called SHOCK Cash Mobs. We arrange and meet with a group of 10 people to each spend £10.00 all at once in a shop or business. The group doesn't know the shop they are going to. Nor does the owner know anything about it. We place ourselves at the centre of the community as a resource for others. Our positivity attracts people to us for advice, support, coffee, cakes and healthy food."

How can a social website help to build our brand?

Firstly, social sites are designed as interactive portals to encourage multiple dialogues. This is between you and your subscribers and between members of your community.

You can provide information to subscribers that could inform, entertain or solve their problems. As a result of the regularly updated information, it increases search engine ranking. This visibility is enhanced because the site enables followers to share your content with other people in their networks.

Social sites are usually built on free platforms such as wordpress.org, wordpress.com and tumblr.com. And the upgrades are usually free or low cost. Also, you can curate content from other sources and integrate them into your site. The combination of viral distribution of your content by followers, search optimisation and generating valuable content will help to create brand awareness.

Developing trust online

We are living in a time when transparency and being personable are essential requirements for developing good communication. Organisations need to show their human face. My Coffee Stop is a good example of this. It's key for you to share views, opinions, information on your various online platforms. These will help to shape your personality and give a clear indication of what your organisation stands for. Other ways to engage with people is to show how you care about them.

Therefore, spend time listening to what they have to say and then responding in a meaningful way. This could be an adjustment in your service due to a complaint from a beneficiary. This will help your end users to feel valued and appreciated. As a result of this your credibility is enhanced because of a practical response to user feedback.

Gaining testimonials from satisfied service users creates another level for building trust. They are very powerful as people want real views about your service, programme or product. A positive profile will enable your reputation to grow. Another offer you can make is to give a guarantee.

Tools you can use to raise your profile

Beyond Facebook, Twitter, YouTube, Instagram and LinkedIn, here are nine other enablers:

- ➢ **Pinterest** – use this tool to collate theme based images around your interests.

- ➢ **Blog** – this acts like an online diary where you share your views, feelings, perspectives and insights on particular matters. You can have conversations with your followers, which in turn builds credibility and trust. Wordpress.org and Tumblr.com are good places to start.

➤ **Google +** – is a social network. The features allow you to categorise your relationships, i.e. friends, acquaintances or add another description. The network also includes a 'Hang Out' feature. This allows you to have video conversations. You can host seminars, deliver training or conduct interviews.

➤ **Friendfeed** – allows you to accumulate all of your online videos, blogs, status updates, photos and bookmarks into one really simple syndication stream (RSS). From this portal you can link up with others in the same way that you do on Twitter.

➤ **Podcasts** – are used to create an audio series around a specific topic. They are really accessible for listeners as they can download them to their computers and smart phones. Therefore, your content becomes portable and can be shared with others. Also, there's the potential to generate revenue from them by selling advertising on them, if you have a large following.

➤ **Slideshare** – let your powerpoint and infographic presentations do your marketing on this platform. Use it to showcase your knowledge and expertise.

➤ **Tinychat** – is a video conference tool that you can use for a seminar with 9 or less people, for free. You can use it as a chat room on your website. Just ask your web designer to help you configure this. Once it's set up, engage with your followers on Twitter and Facebook and invite them into your chat room.

➢ **Ustream** – if you are considering live television as part of your marketing and branding strategy, then you have to sign up for a Ustream account. This allows you to broadcast live across the internet. All you need to kick start your efforts are a microphone and a webcam. Your viewers can connect with each other in the chat room and it also has a feature that enables integration with Twitter.

➢ **Viddler** – this is another video site to host your content that is longer than ten minutes. So if you have an idea for an internet television show or training seminar, then this is a good way forward. Also, you can incorporate your logo and brand colours on your video.

Developing your social media strategy

There are a plethora of social media platforms and there's a temptation to join all of them. When developing your social media strategy, resist joining too many platforms. Examine all your options then give consideration to whether these channels are the right ones for you. Start exploring this by thinking of your audiences and stakeholders and the most likely social media they will use.

Furthermore, research the mediums that your competitors are using. Look out for the levels of interaction between your competitor and their followers. Also, if you notice any trends or positive practices, consider how you can model them.

Once you've made a decision on which channels you are going to focus on, involve staff, trustees and volunteers in communicating your message. Go through a selection process to marry the skills and expertise of each person with the chosen media. For instance, if someone is able to write succinctly, then assign them to Twitter.

Conversely, if other people are confident with visual communication then they could feature in YouTube videos. Choose the right people for each platform then commit to implementing your plan.

How can we measure our return on engagement from our online activities?

Given the expansion of social media tools it's not advisable to have just an overall social media objective. **Cemanthe McKenzie, CEO, New Media Angels,** offers this **practical tip.**

"It's more important to have a Facebook objective, a Twitter objective and so on. This is bcause they are very different platforms with differing outputs.

Some initial questions you can ask yourself are:

1. Which platforms are we going to focus on?
2. What are we going to do on each platform?
3. What is the key objective for each platform?

For example, if you like and friend people on Facebook, what are you hoping to achieve? You need to take both a qualitative and quantitative approach. A return on involvement is more important that return on investment. The involvement could be centred on your social media customer service. And the objective could be to improve customer services."

The time spent listening, engaging and providing solutions will enhance your likeability with your users and other stakeholders. Ultimately, they could go on to spread the word that you are a caring organisation. This is a huge return on your initial engagement as it helps to build brand awareness and equity.

Three other outcomes that can flow from positive online engagement are:

➢ Stronger reputation – this arises because you've demonstrated superior user experience, provided great content, delivered a memorable service and your positive behaviour online.

➢ Increased public relations – due to positioning your organisation as one that positively contributes content and conversation, your social capital, community and reputation grows. Your followers will help to establish you as the go to organisation and will refer their contacts to you.

Furthermore, you can come to the attention of powerful bloggers and journalists.

➤ Organisational insights through building relationships and listening to people online you gain access to the latest trends and intelligence. Having this information will help you make better informed decisions for your organisation. Also, it will help you save time, effort and money.

What are the key things we need to bear in mind as we develop our blog?

A blog is a series of articles that form an online journal that has a global reach. To enhance your blogging activities:

➤ Blog on a regular basis and provide interesting and useful content for your readers. Don't use this platform as a sales pitch. It's good to remember that people search for information so provide them with knowledge they require.

➤ Try to create a heading for your post that can generate a discussion. Posing a question is a good way to attract people and encourage interaction.

➤ Actively engage in dialogue and encourage feedback and opinions. If people disagree with your views, do not respond in a defensive manner.

> ➤ Your blog is another example of your public face, i.e. your brand. Protect it, but don't undermine it.

Managing online conversations

You'll generate so much information online from all of your different platforms that it's useful if you can organise your content. Engagio, is a service that organises online chats from sources such as Twitter, Facebook, Tumblr, LinkedIn, Google + and Foursquare and creates a gmail style, social inbox.

In addition to tracking your discussions Engagio allows you to follow one or more people across all the platforms they use, just with a simple click of a button. This can all be done via the engagement discovery dashboard. This feature in effect extends the management of conversations into a social network.

There is also a facility that helps gmail account users to send updates or tweets to their Facebook, Twitter and Linkedin accounts. You can reply to messages as well as sharing and liking them.

Social media personnel

If you are interested in creating a role for someone to handle your social media activities their key tasks will be to market your message, product service and brand. To help them to do this productively, they should have the following traits:

> ➢ Naturally interested in what everyone does in the organisation and how this impacts on beneficiaries, clients and other stakeholders. Then pull together engaging information.

> ➢ Writes in a conversational voice because the aim is to engage in dialogue between you and your various audiences and between themselves.

> ➢ Responds immediately to questions and comments because creating engagement is critical to followers feeling valued.

> ➢ Clearly understands the organisation's objectives and outcomes in order to distil and convey them in social conversations. This will help to convey what the organisation stands for.

> ➢ Respects confidentiality and knows what the most appropriate information is to reveal to the public.

Beyond the remit of the social media manager, everyone in the organisation should be actively encouraged to become viral brand ambassadors. This will continue to humanise the face of the organisation and bring out its personality.

In addition, everyone is a personal brand so showing your knowledge, passion, expertise and personality is crucial. Particularly in this climate of redundancies and portfolio careers, your personal social footprint is your new resume. One of my favourite business leaders and the godfather of social media, **Gary Vaynerchuk, CEO, Vayner Media** offers this **practical tip.**

"Developing your personal brand is the same thing as living and breathing your resume every second you're working. Your latest tweet, comment on Facebook and most recent blog post are going to announce to the world your ideas and opinions. The very things that make you unique to the world and reveal why a firm would be dumb not to hire you.

Think how different your situation would look if you got laid off but had been keeping up your personal brand and become well known as a hot commodity. Before it would have taken hours of phone calls and emails to announce you're available.

Today, thirty minutes after getting the bad news, you write a blog, send out a tweet and a status update on Facebook about your situation and immediately every manager in your industry would know you're looking for a job and since they'd already be familiar with your brand, think, *"Hmm, how can I get her on board?"* Through your content you are making sure that people get to know you personally and professionally."

Social media...On your way to becoming online moguls

Mini workout

1. Identify the top 3 niche audiences within your beneficiaries and stakeholders.

2. Name the social media tools they use on a regular basis.

3. What are your objectives for each social media tool that you use?

4. Think through strategic and service issues and highlight 5 areas that you could write a blog post on immediately.

5. Undertake a skills' audit with trustees, staff and volunteers to find out each of their strengths that can build your social media strategy.

[6]

Time to raise money
Is it deal or no deal?

Securing finances and resources to deliver services is the number one preoccupation for the leadership team. Yet there are fundraising fundamentals that some still struggle with. Understanding and building upon the following tactics will assist you to expand your funding activities.

A key concern and question of every funder is, "does this organisation have the operational and project management expertise to implement the project proposal?" The reason why they are keen to see this ability demonstrated in a proposal is because the remit of a funder is grant making and not service delivery. Consequently, they rely exclusively on non-profit organisations for execution. Therefore, it's imperative that you define in the proposal the capacity of the organisation to fulfil on the promises made. Omitting this feature basically ensures that your application will be rejected. It will be perceived as a risky service to invest resources into.

Even if you are a new organisation without a track record you can still show your credibility by:

- ➢ Articulating the viability of the service.

- ➢ Providing research that substantiates the need for the service. This could come from a mini pilot scheme, consultation with potential beneficiaries, new legislation or change in government policy.

- ➢ Answering why you are the right organisation who has a suitable solution to an identifiable problem.

- ➢ A quality business model that indicates how the service will actually function, on a day to day basis.

- ➢ A clear revenue model that shows how money will be raised to deliver the service.

- ➢ Aligning the service concept with issues covered in the media.

- ➢ Showcase skills, experience and expertise of all the people involved in developing, managing and leading the organisation.

> Identifying a partner organisation that will support you because they have a successful track record in implementing projects.

What are the main themes that should be included in a fundraising strategy?

Ideally, funding applications should not be developed in response to a sudden shift in any funding criteria that bears no relation to the philosophy or identity of your organisation. Creating a fundraising strategy will bring more coherence to future applications. It will help to sharpen your focus on developing areas of distinction. General questions or themes that should be reflected in the strategy range from:

> How does your organisation distinguish itself from competitors? Because you are operating in a crowded marketplace so you have to find a way to stand out.

> Clearly defined projects and services and the rationale for delivering them.

> An understanding of the world of your service users including their needs, frustrations, hopes and desires. Imagine life in their shoes.

> Justify the range of resources required including human, financial and capital.

> The intellectual assets that could be sold. Comb through the various areas of knowledge and expertise that exists in the organisation. Give consideration to the services or products that could be created based on these assets.

> ➤ Categorise the various ways that could gener-
> ate income namely; trading, commissioning,
> major donors, grants, crowd funding and corpo-
> rate sponsors.

> ➤ Include a list of high net worth individuals who
> are known to the organisation. Think about the
> pitch you could make to them.

**Jan Knight, CEO of Camden Citizen's Advice
Bureau** offers this **practical tip.**

"Before you develop your fundraising strategy, start by
understanding how your finance model works. When I
joined the CAB, overheads were allocated against the
project or contract that was being delivered. However, this
method didn't show us which one of our services was
profitable or running at a loss. You need to know this type
of information so that you evaluate which services to
continue with and which to close down."

Appealing to funders

Although each funder has its own assessment criteria
and priorities there are common elements that they all
look for in proposals. They include:

> ➤ Reflecting current trends, perspectives and
> concerns.

> ➤ Aims to create a level playing field through
> reversing a disadvantage.

> ➤ Has the potential to generate future income.

> ➤ Solves a problem or satisfies an urgent need.

> ➢ Is innovative and achievable.

> ➢ Provides an alternative to what already exists.

Phillip Davis, Programme Manager at Comic Relief offers this **practical tip.**

"To hold the attention of a funder, a funding proposal must be closely aligned to the funding criteria and outcomes. To really understand the funder's perception of the issue pay close attention to their policy documents where you will discover the rationale for why they have developed a particular programme. The proposal must demonstrate how trustees are adept at strategic planning.

Any research and development should give an understanding of what the world may look like in 3, 4, or 5 years' time. And how the organisation could respond to it. Demonstrate professionalism by showing how you run an efficient and streamlined organisation.

The project description should be well written and must be easily understood Funders are not interested in reading proposals that are written like a university thesis. A crucial element of all proposals is that they must give clear evidence of the need for the service. This will be borne out by developing the strategy that reveals that you have scanned the environment, understand and are aware of the policy and legislative changes. And how your proposal fits within it."

Following on from this practical advice here are some errors that must be avoided when you are writing funding applications. Avoid:

> ➢ Emotional language that shows the organisation is desperate for money. This can occur if the focus is on job retention instead of user needs.

> ➢ Jargon, niche phrases or colloquialism.

> ➢ Send audio visual materials like CDs or DVDs.

> ➢ Offer opinions or perspectives instead of facts.

> ➢ Summarise the proposal because you assume the reader is aware of the background and problems you are addressing.

> ➢ Unreferenced research material.

> ➢ Assume one funder will refer your proposal onto another potential funder.

How do we demonstrate the rationale for our project idea?

You can justify the project idea through liaising with your users to discover if they have any emerging needs. These will differ from the ones that you have originally responded to. Also, review the monitoring and evaluation data to see if there are any patterns of change.

Give consideration to what would happen if the problem or situation were left without a solution. Think in terms of the beneficiary, their family and the wider community.

And finally, situate the project idea in the external environment by connecting it to current trends, policies or legislation. Show how these factors support your proposal.

Business support

Seeking funding or other resources from the business community requires you to first build up relationships with key personnel in these companies. And you must be able to answer the question, 'what's in it for them?' How will they benefit from being associated with your organisation? If you have created a strong level of engagement, then the type of support you could receive include:

> ➢ In kind support which ranges from printing costs for your annual report, promoting your service to their customers and clients, donating their products and equipment and offering the use of meeting rooms.

> ➢ Sponsorship of an event, mentorship, pro-gramme, award ceremony or annual lecture series.

> ➢ Multiple year commitments such as funding a scholarship programme for business students for the next five years.

> ➢ Create volunteer opportunities for employees.

> ➢ Provide secondment opportunities for staff.

> ➢ One-off cash donation.

**Edie Fassnidge, Former CSR Manager at the City
of London Local Authority** offers this **practical tip.**

"Voluntary sector organisations need to take a very clear,
concise and direct approach when contacting businesses,
because they receive hundreds of emails every week
asking for support. Therefore, it's useful if organisations
know their elevator pitch specify exactly what they want,
how much it will cost the company, the length of time of the
project, the impact it will have and how the company will
benefit."

**We want to compile a list of business prospects
that may be able to support us, who could we
approach?**

Look for the following types of companies in your local
area as they tend to fall below the gaze of organisations:

> ➢ Architectural firms – could be a match for your
> organisation if you plan on making better use
> of public spaces that will engage local residents

> ➢ Property developers – may not be visible on
> high streets or attend meetings and events that
> usually bring non-profit organisations and
> statutory agencies together. If you require office
> space this could be donated or at a reduced
> rent. Also, they might give a personal donation
> if they have a connection with your mission
> statement.

> Technology companies tend to generate very high profits and may operate a matching gift programme.

> Transport and moving companies such as taxi, removals, ferry, small airlines, bus, rail, trucking / logistics firms.

> Service industries – explore a wide spectrum such as; private retirement communities, pest control, foster care agencies, vet clinics, beauty spas and vending companies.

> Entertainment field spans a range of activities for research namely; dog track, golf courses, casinos, cinemas and bingo halls.

Tim Carr, Director of Community and Social Engagement at Amey, offers this **practical tip.**

"Companies take a number of things into account when considering support to non-profits. The questions that are often posed are; what type of return on investment will we get? How can our business provide a better service as a result of working with non-profits? How can they help us contribute to our local community? And, how can non-profits add value to our business?

For example, organisations should have an awareness of grants that are available to businesses that support local people and their communities. This type of information should be included in a pitch.

Companies need to report to their shareholders who must be protected against exposure to risky investments. Therefore transparent processes are required to prevent any form of misappropriation of money.

> Before approaching a company, do some research to thoroughly understand what it is they do and what their needs are. Companies just don't have the time to explain all of this. Sadly, too often, organisations overlook this responsibility."

What types of benefits accrue to businesses that sponsor non-profit organisations?

The reasons why companies offer sponsorship include:

> ➤ They want to improve their image following a public relations disaster and want to promote their caring compassionate credentials.

> ➤ Generate brand awareness with the communities they serve, which could lead to more customers and profits.

> ➤ Want help to gain exposure for a new product or service and aligning with a non-profit mission statement, could do this.

> ➤ Creates valuable publicity that could help them to attract new target markets.

> ➤ Solidifying relationships with their, suppliers, clients and media companies because non-profits provide an entertainment opportunity because they received sponsorship.

We want to include statutory funding as an income stream. What are some of the things that we should do and avoid?

Statutory funding like any other funding stream should only be pursued if it supports a project idea that flows from user needs supported by documentary evidence. If this is the case then it will be useful for you to understand the bureaucratic decision making structure of central and local government and public agencies.

As an outsider, this can be difficult to navigate. Ways in which you could gain some understanding are by attending public committee meetings. Or become a voluntary sector representative on a multi sector partnership board. Also, cultivate relationships with politicians, on a national or local level. And do the same with decision making staff in the public sector. Relationship building and management are crucial tactics to help you acquire the finances and other resources that are needed.

Think in terms of being a solution provider to the statutory sector who is trying to find answers to certain social and economic problems and priorities. This approach will help you to understand that you are a seller of services who adds value. As opposed to, being an exclusive recipient of grant aid, which is rapidly diminishing.

Implement your media strategy to raise your profile and bring you into the public consciousness. Submit articles, write advertorials or make contact with local radio and television stations to be interviewed. In terms of social media you can approach other blogging platforms to become a guest blogger on their site. You should avoid:

> ➤ Contacting politicians and decision makers at the point that you need support and money.

➤ Assuming that because you may have been funded in the past, this automatically means you'll be funded again in the future.

➤ Being modest in terms of what your organisation can do.

➤ Presenting out of date information.

➤ Short term planning.

What does leverage mean? And how can we show it in our fundraising activities?

Leverage is a practice that enables a small contribution of support to be expanded to create maximum impact for your beneficiaries. It can happen in a variety of ways such as:

➤ Match funding takes place when a funder agrees to contribute half the cost that is required. And you still have the responsibility to raise the balance.

➤ Lasting impact on the lives of your beneficiaries, way beyond the time frame of when they received the service from you.

➤ Saving money and other resources because your service or product has solved a problem for your beneficiaries. And as a result of this, local and central government and the wider public do not have to deal with the consequences or spend additional money.

> Using volunteers to help deliver your projects can add more value than if just paid staff are used. This is because volunteer participation enhances their lives as well as beneficiaries. Also their involvement could assist in gaining employment and develop their own business or go back to education.

> Challenge grants are only secured when you've entered into an agreement with a donor that they will pay half the money requested. This is only if you raise the rest of it by a certain date. If you are unsuccessful, the donor doesn't pay anything.

How do we define our unique selling point?

One way in which you can best describe your unique selling point is to stand in the position of your beneficiaries and then think about all the benefits they'll receive from your organisation. To gain a better understanding of what the benefits are you could create a list of similar services / products in your niche sector and identify gaps that are unsatisfied needs.

For example, service users may want a; faster service, better prices, excellent quality, convenience, personal service or a better guarantee. You could distinguish yourself from competitors by including one or more of these factors into your service or product.

Another way you can create a unique selling point is by marketing an aspect of your service that isn't necessarily unique, but is unknown to your beneficiaries and stakeholders. For instance, does your service use a method or process that assures a quality experience for all your service users? Using the power of storytelling about this could   produce a unique feature / unique selling point.

Throughout the usage of your unique selling point you must take steps to update it. Otherwise, it will become stale in the minds of your beneficiaries. And your competitors may replicate the best features of it.

Action checklist for fundraising activities

Compiling the following in a coherent and accessible way, will help to organise your planned fundraising projects:

> ➢ Background information of the organisation governing documents, vision and mission statements, aims, objectives and rationale for starting.

> ➢ The main successes and achievements of the organisation and names of financial backers.

> ➢ List of testimonials, endorsements and media coverage.

> ➢ Any case studies and research data that will help to bolster your position on why you are best suited to deliver services and provide solutions.

> ➢ A fundraising strategy.

> ➢ Information on the proposed projects.

> ➢ Budget information.

> ➤ People in your network who can assist in your fundraising endeavours.

In addition, **Ian Redding, Former Head of Grants at London Councils** offers this **practical tip.**

"Voluntary and community organisations need to diversify their fundraising activities. They should develop clarity around how all their services link into the funding strategy, by making strategic decisions. For example, they may decide that there are certain activities they will always deliver and it may be more appropriate to approach a socially orientated trust. Rather than a local business for support.

With regards to sustainability, organisations should always be asking; Are we still relevant? What are the policy changes that are taking place? What are the new pressures that our users are experiencing?

And if they are going to find different ways to resource their organisation then they need to understand the new funding direction. Once they know this, they must learn how to position themselves to take advantage of it."

Crowd funding

Following on the suggestion of a new funding direction, crowd funding is a viable alternative. Essentially, this is an online financing option that brings together fund-raisers and donors or investors.

The way in which the process works is once you've designed a very short organisational story and pitch, of about three minutes, you record a video and upload it onto the crowd funding platform. The video must also include how much money you want to raise.

If people like your idea they will make a contribution. And if you reach your target amount within a specific timeframe, then you will be awarded all the money. If not, then you don't receive anything. These platforms tend to operate on an all or nothing basis.

The type of financing that is available are, loans, donations, equity or rewards. Nesta, the funder and investment charity has produced a Crowd Funding Directory it contains information about 31 different platforms. You can download a copy of the directory from www.crowdingin.com

Time to raise money...Is it deal or no deal?

Mini workout

1. What are the 3 main policies and /or laws that impact on your service area?

2. Write a 1 page profile of your board of trustees highlighting how their skills and expertise enhance the organisation.

3. Identify 3 frustrations that your beneficiaries experience. How will your organisation help them to overcome them?

4. How is your organisation different from your top 3 competitors?

5. Name 3 actions you will take to enhance your relationship with a current funder and a potential donor.

[7]

It's the swipe economy
Let your apps do the talking

Static websites are still in vogue. However, mobile platforms are leading the way in terms of how we all communicate our brands, messages, stories products and services. And a mobile application is the software that enables us to do this on smart phones, tablet computers and other mobile devices.

Apps are an efficient way to convey information that can help people improve their lives, entertain and educate them, as well. In addition to this they are a money making device. So this marketing tool can be an income generation stream for your organisation.

The three main operating platforms for Apps are; Apple IOS, Google Android and RIM. Apple is the most recognised platform and it is the market leader. So it's easier to create apps for the iPhone, iPad and iPod because of compatible hardware.

What to look for when designing an app

Before rushing off into the design phase of an app, you must have an understanding of your marketplace, customer needs and desires. The Apple App Store is the best place for you to start to conduct your research for trends, common features of successful apps, changes in revenue models from free to paid ones.

To help you keep abreast of market developments follow Apple's list of the top paid, top free and top grossing apps. The type of questions you should be asking as you review the lists are:

- ➢ Why is this app great?

- ➢ What do customers say about it?

- ➢ Why would people pay for it?

- ➢ What is the unique selling point of this app?

- ➢ What are the marketing tactics used by the developers to attract customers?

You can evaluate the likeability of an app by considering whether it is engaging, entertaining and brings joy to the user. Visually, it should be easy on the eye and the audio should be high quality. Also, it should be so engaging that customers can't wait to come back and use it. Lastly, it should be appealing to a wide range of people.

Characteristics of a good app developer

When you are ready to hire an app developer, you can assess their suitability by reviewing their portfolio of apps to assess the quality of their work. Here you're looking for clarity and sharpness of the visuals and functionality of the app.

In terms of finding developers speak to friends and people in your network to gain personal recommendations. Or review websites such as www.odesk.com, www.elance.com and www.freelancer.com.These outsourcing site will have reviews based on developers' previous work. You also want to check that they have good communication skills including the ability to explain technicalities in layman terms. They should be responsive to changing requirements. If a developer can write code as well as design, then this is a winning combination. If you have difficulty in finding this combination then you need to be working with a programmer and graphic designer.

What type of questions should we be asking during the initial assessment stage?

Here's a selection:

- ➢ How many apps have you created?

- ➢ Can I look at your designs?

- ➢ Can I have the names of 3 references?

- ➢ What are some of the things that frustrate you when working with clients?

- ➢ How do you resolve the frustration?

- ➢ Do you work with a team? If so, what are their skills?

- ➢ How do you ensure you don't compete with your clients?

- ➢ What process do you use to submit an app to the App Store?

- ➢ If you become ill during our project, do you have a network of designers and programmers who can support you?

- ➢ Can you identify performance indicators that are linked to payments?

When you've completed the interview, let them know if you choose to move forward with them, they will be required to sign a non-disclosure agreement. Only after this formality should you discuss the idea of your app.

Marketing your app

The features that will draw the attention of users are the icon, title, description and the screenshots. The icon is the visual representation of your app. It has to be attractive enough and in that single image it must convey the core principle of the app. When your target audience comes across it, they must know that it relates to them.

In relation to the title choose one that gives a clear description of what the app does. Also, bear in mind that it should in some way be searchable as a keyword. People generally search for answers to questions, queries, problems and to satisfy a need. When you are considering the description of your app, use a strap line for the opening sentence. This should be followed by a few sentences highlighting the benefits then concluded with a call to action.

Lastly, all the screenshots should provide a summary of what customers will encounter when they engage with your app. Screenshots are conveyed as images, so tell your story in five images.

Nag screen

This is an extra promotional tool that helps to entice a user to select a premium version of a free app they have previously downloaded. It's a pop up window that appears when an app is opened. Basically you are presenting a sales opportunity for them to buy another version of the app which has more features.

You can also use nag screens to promote other apps that you have created. Whatever content you include in this screen focus it towards the benefits the user will receive.

What other methods can we use to promote our app?

Three other tactics that you can implement are promotional pages, push notifications and your networks. The benefit of using a promotional page is that it enables you to cross promote multiple apps at the same time. Through this page users can read reviews and access the app.

To increase the click through rate, put a visible 'more button' on the app. You are aiming to generate a number of potential customers, some who will respond to your call to action, which will lead to sales.

Another technique you can use is push notices. They function in a similar way to text messaging. Send notices to people who already have your app on their phone. This micro billboard is a powerful way for you to continue building a relationship with your customers.

However, be mindful about not coming across as spamming.

Also, you can learn so much about app development by following bloggers in the tech arena. A useful site to visit is www.techcrunch.com. As with any blog the key is to create interaction, so ask questions, post comments and build relationships. And attend technology conferences, seminars and research a Meetup Group in your area. If one doesn't exist, then set one up.

What's the difference between a free, premium and freemium app?

The lead generator for creating sales or marketing your message is a free app. You can use banner advertising, affiliate marketing and translated versions of your app to create an income. Free apps are also an easy way for potential customers to familiarise themselves with your brand.

The premium revenue model caters for all paid apps. Here you can also utilise affiliate marketers to sell the app on your behalf, for a pre-agreed percentage of the sale. Furthermore, features are included that are used to entice customers to buy more advanced usage.

The freemium model is a combination of free and premium apps. It includes an option to upgrade to receive paid content. This is already built into the app therefore users do not have to go back to the App Store to buy it.

A tactic that should be used in your revenue strategy is banner advertising. The reason for this is the growing trend amongst advertisers that are moving away from traditional advertising mediums. This is due to the rise in the alternative digital and mobile platforms that consumers are gravitating towards.

How can banner advertising help us to increase sales?

Advertisers are spending more of their marketing budgets on engaging with their audiences who use mobile devices. They buy advertising space on mobile ad networks. If you use your apps to display adverts you will receive 60% of the ad revenue that comes from this process. The remaining balance goes to the advertising networks. You'll actually make money every time one of the adverts is clicked or displayed.

The three main advertising networks to use when you want to integrate ads inside you app are; Apple's iAd, Google's Admob and Millenial Media. These platforms can be used separately or you can request adverts from all three. The best service to use to help you integrate all three is Ad Whirl which is provided by Google.

At what stage should we consider translating our app into another language?

The best time to start translating your app is once it has been established in your home market and other English speaking countries. The major ones are the U.K. America, Canada and Australia. The key elements to be translated are the; title, description, keywords and screenshots.

Hire native speakers to undertake the translation because they have the greatest appreciation of the nuances in the language. All of your marketing information must be aligned with the best interpretation.

Outside of English-speaking territories, then consider translating your app in Mandarin, French and Spanish-speaking countries. Also, pay attention to developments in emerging markets.

Future trends

The research company, Gartner Inc, predict the following trends in the app industry. Knowing these predictions, imagine, with a shift in strategy, where your organisation could be in 18 months' time.

Location based services – i.e. services based on current geographic location	Context aware services – i.e. customising services based on personal interests.
Social networking – i.e. web conversations and photo-sharing	Object recognition – i.e. based on surroundings
Mobile search – i.e. integrate information searches	Mobile instant messaging – i.e. include interactive features
Mobile commerce – i.e. buying things	Mobile email – i.e. use phones to send more emails
Mobile payment – i.e. by mobile phone.	Mobile video – i.e. phone and video services will work together to deliver high definition videos to mobile phones.

It's the swipe economy
Let your apps do the talking

Mini workout

1. Following research on the Apple App Store, what are 3 leading trends in the market you want to create an app in?

2. Describe the unique selling point of the app that you want to design.

3. Choose a title for your app that would be easy for people to find using a keyword search.

4. What message would you use in a nag screen to encourage a user to buy an upgrade in your app?

5. Select 3 areas from the Gartner predications, which you could develop a bundle of apps to satisfy emerging needs of your beneficiaries.

[8]

Marketing your message
Do you know who you're talking to?

There are approximately 165,000 registered charities, voluntary and community organisations in England and Wales and thousands of unregistered non-profit organisations. And together they are busy delivering services to the following causes, as outlined by www.charitytrends.org namely, disability, environment, sports / recreation, relief of poverty, housing, arts / culture, religious activities, community development/employment, medical / health, education / training, animals, armed forces and general charitable purposes.

The ratio of the total number of organisations and the number of causes demonstrates that you are operating in crowded markets. So what do you need to do to raise your profile? Become effective marketers.

Marketing is the ability and act of storytelling that creates emotional engagement with your listener, viewer or reader. **Joel Roberts, a Media and Communications Genius**, shares the view that:

"As marketers we need to understand how to get heard in a crowded market place. We need to brand out from the crowd. Essentially, we have to stand up, stand out and sell!"

However, before any selling takes place you have to become adept at creating and communicating the narrative of your organisation and the strategic and operational stories that flow out from it. The reason for this is that stories have an emotional centre and show us what it is to be human. Engaging emotions is the catalyst to drawing stakeholders to your cause, services, activities, products and projects.

Throughout our lives we have been exposed to story-telling. But are you aware of the range of story formats that can help you craft your stories? If not, take account of the following table as stated by, **Phil Parker, Author and Director of Not Your Average Company**

The Romance	Romeo in Romeo and Juliet
The Unrecognised Virtue	The prostitute in Pretty Woman
The Fatal Flaw	Dr. Ross in E.R.

The Debt that must be Repaid	Del Boy in Only Fools and Horses
The Gift that is Taken Away	Tennyson in Prime Suspect
The Quest	Luke in Star Wars
The Rites of Passage	Muriel in Muriel's Wedding
The Wanderer	Thelma in Thelma and Louise
The Spider and The Fly	Valmont in Dangerous Liaisons
The Character who cannot be Put Down	Conan in Conan the Barbarian

Whichever phase of development your organisation is at you can start pulling together the elements of its story. Defining your elevator pitch is a way to start building your story.

Elevator pitch

The myth around an elevator pitch is that it was born in the elevators on Wall Street, in New York. The idea is that you should be able to encapsulate succinctly who you are, what you do, who you serve and who you want to meet within a 20-second timeframe. Therefore, anyone who enquires about you is able to comprehensively understand what your brand stands for.

"During networking events you have to cut through the noise to grab someone's attention. Because we offer specialist business information, I say, you can't afford not to speak to me." **Goretti Considine, Former Director, City Business Library**

It's useful to put your pitch on the back of your business card as it acts as a 24 hour avatar. And is a way to jog someone's memory about your organisation.

Point of view

Your business card could lead you to presenting your story to a business audience who are keen to support charities. There are different points of view in which you can tell the story. If you think about the basics of storytelling there is a protagonist or hero. This character will help to establish a point of view for your listeners. In relation to organisations, you can choose from six organisational heroes namely; the person telling the story, the listener, beneficiary, product / service, location or community. Before you select the hero decide what you want to achieve as a result of the presentation. Identify your objectives.

For instance, if you want the audience to have confidence in your abilities as the CEO, then assume the hero position. Show how you are effectively leading the organisation. If you're inviting the audience to take a perceived risk, i.e. to invest in a new initiative, then show them as the hero. Or, if you want to enhance your brand over your competitors, then the service / product or location, becomes the hero. And if you want the audience to promote and support your programme of activities, then highlight the community as the hero.

What type of content should we use in our stories?

You can craft your content from a wide range of sources including; personal experiences from your service users, observations within your cultural, social, political and local communities. In addition to using metaphors and information from the whole world of subjects i.e. science, technology, business and anthropology. You can also incorporate ideas from books, mythology and history as sources of inspiration. Whichever you choose, design them around the journey of your objectives, outputs and outcomes that you are aiming to achieve.

Compelling call to action

If you have caught the attention of your audience you have succeeded in stirring their emotions through the story that has activated their desire to respond. This could be out of frustration, wanting to reverse an injustice or needing to make a contribution because they've experienced the benefit of such an act. It is imperative to guide them to take the action that is required to buy into your vision. Your call to action should be structured to connect to what could be their motivators.

Promote benefits

It is important to promote the benefits of your services and products instead of their features. The reason for this is that your primary goal for marketing is to create a meaningful connection with the recipients of what you have to offer. By promoting the benefits you are demonstrating that you have an understanding of what their problem is and the benefits of your offering shows a clear solution to the problem. Benefits are about the impact you want them to experience. Benefits speak to the effects of what you have to offer, e.g. 'join our cooking and healthy eating programme and lose a stone in weight over the next twelve weeks.'

If you advertise the features over and above the benefits you are describing what the service is and how it functions. E.g. 'our weekly cooking classes are delivered in children's centres by trainee chefs from local colleges. Through step by step practical demonstrations, they teach you how to prepare nutritious meals.'

Therefore, when designing your marketing messages give consideration to how you can create rewarding experiences for the people you want to engage with your product or service. If you are a new organisation you won't have a track record, you may be thinking, what can we use to market ourselves? Four attributes that can be used are:

> ➤ The expertise, experience and knowledge of the board of trustees.

> ➤ The innovative service solutions you intend to provide to solve the problems of your beneficiaries.

> ➤ Personal awards received by trustees, i.e. fellowships.

> ➤ Your mission statement and the story that surrounds why the organisation was established.

Andy Gregg, CEO of Race on the Agenda offers this practical tip.

"Organisations should have a theory of change in terms of what they want their marketing activities to achieve. Think through what you do, how you do it and what type of change do you want to create at a macro level. It's vital to know why people may want to work with or support your organisation. You must have an answer to this. At times, project funding can undermine your attempt to have a coherent brand therefore it's important that you are able to reconcile these positions."

Mission statement upgrade

A mission statement encompasses the heart of your intentions. However, it tends to be written in a dry, academic way with very little emotional engagement. It should aim to capture the attention of your audience and stir their emotions. A mission statement can be revitalised by approaching the task with a marketing mindset. Providing answers to the following three questions can help to reshape it:

> ➢ Why does your organisation continue to exist?

> ➢ What are the key principles that connect your organisation's central purpose?

> ➢ What are the key outcomes that your organisation wants to achieve?

While reviewing your mission statement, give some thoughts to what can help you establish a competitive advantage. This is important as you want to distinguish yourself from other organisations. And be memorable in the minds of your stakeholders.

You can appear more appealing to them by distinguishing yourself in the following ways; the niche market you cater for, the type of service on offer, the quality and speed of delivery of the service, how convenient it is for people to acquire and access your service, the price you charge, (if applicable) and the type of marketing campaign that you run.

Differences between traditional and guerrilla marketing

Traditional and guerrilla marketing are two approaches to bring your message to the public. By understanding the extent of your resources including money, people, energy and time, you will know which strategy to apply to your situation. Five key distinctions between the two marketing methods are:

➢ Those who practice traditional marketing tend to invest money in advertising. Whereas, guerrilla marketers prefer to use their time, energy and imagination to find effective ways to connect to their market.

➢ Organisations that continually push their messages onto audiences, market in a traditional way. It's just a procession of one way dialogue. Conversely, guerrilla marketers engage in a dialogue and build relationships with people. This interactive process helps to build trust and confidence in your brand.

➢ Guerrilla marketers use psychology to try and understand why people use their services or buy their products. Alternatively, traditional marketers base their strategy on past experience and their judgement.

> ➤ Traditional marketing aims to eliminate competition. Guerrilla marketing is about collaboration to bring about a win-win situation.

> ➤ Guerrilla marketing uses a variety of tools simultaneously. Traditional marketing relies on one method at a time to communicate to its audience.

Where can we find free marketing opportunities?

Five activities that you can get involved with that will help your marketing strategy are:

> ➤ Join associations and clubs as they are gateways to finding out inside market information. It leads to connections with movers and shakers in your sector. This could lead to finding new partners, referrals, suppliers, clients and journalists, who could also tell you story.

> ➤ Write articles for newsletters, newspapers and magazines that add value and solve problems for the readership. This is also a great way to demonstrate your expertise. Also it will help to build your credibility.

> ➤ Give talks at other non-profit organisations and professional associations. They provide platforms to increase your visibility while you share valuable insights. However, don't use this opportunity to deliver a sales pitch.

> ➤ Join online forums because these discussion groups help to build your presence through

dialogue with people from across the world. Provide answers to questions that have been posted. Look at yourself as a resource to help others. This will help to build trust and from here a whole range of benefits will arise.

➢ Use community bulletin boards to spread your message.

Effective networking

Marketing tactics will also involve staff, volunteers and trustees attending seminars, meetings or events, to spread the word about what you're doing. Beforehand, discuss and plan what it is that you want to achieve by attending, e.g. do you want to identify potential future partners? Or connect with journalists as you have newsworthy information? Or to meet a high net worth individual who could be a future donor? The underlying question that you must answer is 'how can our organisation serve or be a benefit to the people we want to connect with?'

Think about what you're going to say to the people who you meet. Practice your introduction, elevator pitch and interesting questions you want to ask. Come prepared with business cards and any other promotional materials. Find out whether the people you meet are open to having a further discussion or meeting. Follow up with them within 48 hours, after meeting them.

Online support

Compliment your offline marketing activities with using the internet to support your work. Seven ways you could incorporate the use of the internet in your organisation to continue marketing are:

- ➤ Deliver online training courses to educate your stakeholders.

- ➤ Carry out research on your target audience, competitors and supporters.

- ➤ Live stream fundraising events.

- ➤ Collect donations online.

- ➤ Provide ongoing advocacy updates.

- ➤ Develop a global presence.

- ➤ Obtain feedback from your beneficiaries.

So you now know that marketing is about engaging storytelling around your service or product. But how do you remain in the minds of potential stakeholders? Well that's where publicity comes in. Let's take a look at how that happens.

Marketing your message
Do you know who you're talking to?

Mini workout

1. Name 1 major event that has happened in the life of a beneficiary and an issue that led to a change in strategy.

2. Which story format will you choose to structure your story?

3. What's your elevator pitch?

4. Name 4 benefits that your service offers?

5. Review your mission statement and rewrite it as a persuasive marketing statement.

[9]

Publicity...If Sir Richard Branson can do it, so can we!

I really enjoyed reading Sir Richard Branson's book, Screw It, Let's Do It Expanded – Lessons in Life and Business. It's full of so many nuggets and one that pertains to this chapter is around publicity. In the early days following the launch of his magazine, Student, he worked hard to gain coverage in the media and received glowing reviews in a range of papers including the Financial Times. Branson offers this **practical tip.**

"This was fantastic publicity and one of the reasons I have spent much of my life being happy about promoting myself and Virgin. Advertising, publicity, promotion call it what you will – works. There is so

much competition in the world, that if you have something to sell, no matter what, you have to get noticed.
It's no use producing goods or having the best ideas
in the universe if they just stayed in your head or
stacked up in the corner of your bedroom."

Developing a media strategy

To gain the attention of media outlets your organisation
has to develop a story hook that's appealing enough
for them to want to interview you. Hooks appear in a
variety of forms and your story should include at least
one of the following:

> ➢ Broadcasters are keen to share breaking news
>   with their audience.

> ➢ The story should be topical and connect with an
>   issue that's currently happening in the world.

> ➢ The story will attract wider appeal if it relates in
>   some way to health, well-being, sex and
>   money.

> ➢ The media likes to entertain and educate its
>   audiences by disproving conventional ideas
>   and shattering myths.

> ➢ If your information teaches people something
>   because it takes an innovative approach to a
>   problem it will appeal to broadcasters.

> ➢ Think of benefits you can offer to an audience.

> Consider how your story is emotionally engaging by fuelling feelings like happiness, empathy or sorrow.

> Connecting your story to a public figure or celebrity will be of interest to the media.

"The media like personal triumph over tragedy stories, find beneficiaries who are prepared to be photographed, tell their story and speak about the issues. Another approach is to send out a survey with a catchy headline. It's worth doing because it could catch someone's attention." **Marina Catacuzino, Founder, The Forgiveness Project**

You can expand upon the strategy by including preparations to be interviewed. First identify 5 key areas that you want to be covered and under each heading create 3-4 subsections. After this, you want to strengthen you're your 5 main areas by adding, for example, case studies, examples, vignettes, and jokes that are evocative, interesting and memorable. Then follow this up by thinking of questions the interviewer may ask about the organisation, the person being interviewed, your product, service, solution and developments in your sector.

What is a media list?

Essentially this is your database of all your contacts who can help to promote your story, product or service. Aim to create a large pool of potential promoters as the response rate to press releases tends to be relatively low. Therefore, sending it out to a large group will increase your chance of someone responding to your story.

Start building your list by collecting names and details of people who specialise in your niche area. Include a wide range such as; bloggers, podcasters, journalists, reporters, writers, producers and editors. The information you collate should include names, full contact details, social media addresses, area of interest your point of reference for knowing this person, their hobbies, interests, mutual friends and acquaintances.

Building media relationships

The media world is a relationship business. Therefore, take your time to develop them, instead of immediately trying to sell them your story. Journalists, bloggers and editors like to see some type of track record. This is in terms of what others have written about individuals in your organisation or about your service or product. If you've been interviewed on the radio, television or on a podcast, give producers a list of the programmes you have been on and provide them with a list of recordings.

Before pitching your idea, clarify the audience you want to reach and research the programmes, magazines, news-papers and bloggers who have the listeners, readers or viewers you want to connect with. Tailor your approach to reflect how your idea will directly benefit the audience - their followers. Also remember to send your proposal to the right person and section that represents the theme you want to discuss. Your story needs to be emotive enough for people to care about. Is it something they will discuss at lunchtime, on forums, send tweets, write comments on Facebook or blog about? If you envisage people engaging around your story that shows it is newsworthy.

Excerpt of a case study on building a relationship with the media

Caroline Criado-Perez a feminist campaigner and the Founder of The Women's Room, which was set up in response to two radio programmes on the BBC's Today Show. The programmes focused on women's issues that were being discussed by men. The presenter claimed they tried to find female experts but were unable to. On hearing this Caroline sent out tweets and twenty women responded immediately. In her view the BBC weren't trying hard enough, so she set up a database in response, so it would become impossible for them to do this again.

On the day she set up the database she contacted journalists who she thought would be sympathetic to the cause. Yvonne Roberts from The Observer immediately saw the worth in what Caroline and her colleagues were doing. She wrote an article about them and it appeared a week later. The Women's Room was set up in response to a particular problem and presents a solution that had just been reported on in the media. As the solution focuses on a contemporary issue, it made it easier for the story to be reported on.

If a news story has the potential for sub topics to flow from it, then give some thoughts on how you could position your organisation within it. For instance a story about torrential rain and flooding could generate stories about health and safety, impact on communities, death, bereavement, changes in weather patterns and the environment. If your organisation links to any of these topics, find the connection and share your narrative.

Writing a good headline

The purpose of a headline is to convey the whole meaning of a story in a concise sentence. Open any newspaper or magazine or newsletter and headlines just jump out at us. A vivid three word headline I recall was on the front page of Time Magazine, it read, 'Man, Superman, Gunman.' The focus of the story was around Oscar Pistorius and the shooting of his girlfriend. This is a tragic story with a compelling headline.

To compose a great headline you should first write the article or story, because the headline should just flow from it. Don't super-impose a headline to fit the article or story.

This principle is similar to when you're writing a business plan. The one or two page executive summary that is at the beginning of the plan acts as the headline for the whole document and is written once it has been completed. Secondly, when preparing the article think about your rationale for writing it. Why is it important that your intended readers should care about what you have to say?

Thirdly, give consideration to what it is that you actually want them to do as a result of reading your information. Give clear guidance about the 'call to action.' When you've compiled your story, you now want to create a bite-size version, which will be your headline.

The key factors that will help to shape the headline are precision and brevity.

> ➢ Precision – we live in a world of information overload and as a result of this your communication has to stand out. Therefore, headlines should not be a conundrum. Readers should not have to think what the story is about. Simplicity is the way forward.

> ➢ Brevity – as the maxim goes, 'less is more' is so appropriate when writing headlines. This is because the key words should provide a snapshot of the story and entice readers to continue. If the headline is too long and unwieldy then you are in danger of turning off the attention of your target audience.

Preparing a press release

Your aim for writing a press release is to grab the attention of media personnel in the world of print, radio and television. As well as consumers who are looking for your solution online. Ideally, your story should fit on one page. To ensure people read the whole page, write a compelling headline that piques the curiosity in your reader so they want to find out more.

To help you sharpen your writing, take time to review magazine and newspaper headlines. Study the composition of the sentence, its tone and how words are used to engage you. Follow the headline with some bullet point sub-headings and a couple of sentences each that build story in terms of priority information that you think they should know.

As you are composing your press release continually ask, 'why is it important for my audience to a care about this story? At the end of the press release include all your contact information and a word count.

What do we need to include in our media kit?

Your media kit is an essential communication package for your media contacts. Here's a checklist of what it should include to showcase your organisation in the best possible light.

➢ A persuasive mission statement that anchors the organisation in terms of what it actually does, clear description of the beneficiaries and how the work of the organisation has a positive impact on their lives.

➢ Biographical information on your board members and staff. When compiling this section includes key attributes about them. These factors should show how their strengths enhance the organisation.

➢ Press release about a worthy piece of news about the organisation. This should just be a page of information and where possible link it to a topical subject that's in the news.

➢ Service related tips that can help your target audiences.

➢ Key facts about the organisation that highlights the problems it solves for its users.

➢ Government and industry policy papers. Provide a summary of the main initiatives that frames your area of service provision.

➢ Description of services, projects, programmes and products.

➢ Positive impact case studies that demonstrate how the organisation has helped to add value to service users.

➢ Latest annual report.

> ➢ Information of published articles both on and offline.

Blogs

Blogs are another tool that can assist you to gain more publicity. By generating excellent content for your readers it will show that the organisation is an expert in the sector. Furthermore they are a great way to promote conversations with and among your readers. It can also be used as a consultation tool that allows you to receive immediate feedback from your followers.

Other benefits include blogs being used as a mechanism to increase your presence in online search engines. This in turn creates awareness of your existence and generates traffic. They are also a useful way to get publicity by engaging with other bloggers and asking them to publish your information on their blogs. Depending on the extent of your relationship, this could be free or you pay a fee. In addition, you have the potential to increase your following by posting comments and answering on other people's blogs.

How do we set up a blog?

Two highly recognised blogging platforms are wordpress.org and tumblr.com. Buy the domain name of what you want to call your blog. It's best if you acquire the .com and .tv. The .com has worldwide recognition and the .tv can be used if you want to create a video blog. You can self-host your blog by using your domain name and setting it up with your hosting company. Or it can be hosted by Wordpress or Tumblr. The URL will look like:

<u>http://mynameis.tumblr.com</u> or
<u>http://mynameis.wordpress.org</u>.

In terms of what your blog looks like you can choose either one of the free themes that are available. If you choose this route just bear in mind that there are other blogs that will look similar to yours. Alternatively, work with a web designer to create a specific look.

Although you can use wordpress.org to upload video, text and photos, tumblr.com has simplified the process because it has created a format for the medium you want to use. This covers audio, text, email, video and photo. Once your content has been uploaded, you just press the 'create post' button.

Organisational book

If your organisation has been delivering services over a period of time, it has gathered a lot of knowledge, insights and perspectives since it started.

Within this information lies valuable intelligence that could be very useful to your beneficiaries, stakeholders and other sectors or industries. Packaging the knowledge into a book creates leverage in your sector by helping to raise brand identity and expertise. It also enhances your credibility, creates a powerful marketing tool and is a calling card for online and offline media. You will be sought out for interviews.

Furthermore, this can lead to speaking engagements and will begin to attract followers at conferences, seminars and on your blog. Lastly, it is a tangible product that can generate unrestricted income.

Publicity...If Sir Richard Branson can do it, so can we!

Mini workout

1. What do you currently do to generate publicity for your organisation? Name 3 additional activities that will help to build or extend your profile.

2. Within the current services you deliver, are there any stories that could be of interest to the media?

3. Who are the leading bloggers and journalists in your niche sector?

4. What would you include in a summary page on relevant government initiatives and policies that impact on your work?

5. If you were invited to be interviewed on a local radio station next week, how would you prepare for it?

[10]

Selling Skills...We might even impress Lord Alan Sugar

Every day you are selling aspects and attributes of your organisation. For example, your pitch might be about acquiring facilities to enable disabled children to participate in sports. Or it could be liaising with other organisations to buy into a vision of collaboration, to deliver more services to people in need. Or, as in the case of the chef, activist and Technology, Entertainment and Design (T.E.D.) 2010 prize winner, Jamie Oliver, who is travelling the world enrolling, governments, companies, communities and individuals with the following vision:

"I wish for everyone to help create a strong sustainable movement to educate every child about food, inspire families to cook again and empower people everywhere to fight obesity."

Beyond products and services you may be just like Jamie in that you are selling an idea, behaviour, belief, attitude or outcome. There are a number of things you need to be aware of before you can achieve the call to action you are seeking.

Build rapport

Everyone in your organisation is a brand advocate. And as a result of this, a core function of their role is to create an affinity, trust and understanding with your potential buyers. A way in which you can do this is to create ongoing opportunities for staff, volunteers and trustees to demonstrate their expertise regarding the organisation's values, the quality of its services and products. Their expertise should be packaged as an educational experience as opposed to a one-dimensional sales pitch. A couple of questions that they can think through to bring about a learning inter-action are:

> ➢ How does this information add value to their lives?

> ➢ How can I help them succeed in their endeav-ours?

Three other suggestions to help better engagement are; finding areas of mutual interest, asking great questions and demonstrating good listening skills. All of these aspects will show that your advocates are really interested in what the person is sharing about their world. Demonstrating empathy for a person's situation is a way to show that you genuinely care.

How do we qualify buyers?

In order to determine if you have a potential buyer, there are two areas you should clarify. They are the needs of your buyers and the criteria they use to assess whether they purchase a product or service or buy into your vision. Devise some key questions that will help to discover more about them. Here are three example questions that you can ask if selling to other organisations:

> ➤ What are 4 things that your organisation is struggling with that affects service delivery?

> ➤ What criteria do you use to decide whether to buy a product or service like ours?

> ➤ What are the key outcomes that your organisation has set out to achieve?

All of your advocates should be trained to ask your core questions to gain a better appreciation of your prospects. As ultimately, your goal here is to provide solutions to their problems.

So for example, public sector commissioners use the following criteria to buy services; a clear social mission, strong management team, ability to deliver social outcomes and the ability to manage complex monitoring processes. Knowing this type of information can help you build an effective proposition that delivers solutions and saves the government money.

Using the organisation's story to add value

The proposition needs to flow from the core story. Here you may choose to paint a picture of your beneficiaries' desires, difficulties, barriers to success and their vision of leading positive lives. This information is blended with market data. Both aspects will strengthen your presentation because you are connecting emotions with facts, which helps to solidify engagement with your audience. And by providing a solution that helps beneficiaries to transition to a new reality can demonstrate how they can participate more effectively in society.

Excerpt from the Channel 4 television programme, The Secret Millions, featuring Kids Company and Gok Wan

The core story of the programme is about transforming the lives of marginalised and disadvantaged young people. The story was embedded in and conveyed effectively in an innovative pilot project. Gok Wan worked with eight young people in a job skills training initiative.

They created and branded a company Breaking the Chain, and undertook market research, designed and produced a

T-shirt and sold it in JD Sports. The twist in the programme was that none of the young people knew that the initiative was being monitored by the Big Lottery Fund, who planned to invest £2m in Kids Company, if the pilot was successful. The Big Lottery Fund was convinced that the initiative would make a difference and Kids Company received the investment.

Three key selling areas that I picked up that Kids Company focused on were:

- They sold the idea to their young people that they are achievers and valuable members of society who are worthy of getting a job. Some changes in behaviour would help achieve this goal.

- They sold the outcome to the Big Lottery Fund that young people from disadvantaged backgrounds can be guided into participating in the workforce, with the right package of support.

- Selling the T-shirts in JD Sports. As a result of this product it has created a new revenue stream for Kids Company. All the proceeds from the sale of the T-shirts go back to the charity. This in turn strengthens their sustainable model.

What is one thing we can do to create a desire to entice people to buy from us?

Focus on delivering a service that creates a notable experience for customers. Too often organisations and companies compete on price with no guarantee on providing a good service. The ways in which you sell your service include:

> ➢ Demonstrating the efficient way in which you supply your service on time.

> ➢ Creating methods that make it easy for customers, beneficiaries and other stakeholders to connect and communicate with your organisation.

> ➢ Having a listed customer service telephone number and an internet phone ID on Skype.

> ➢ Deliver on all the promises that were made when your customer bought your product or service.

What type of objections could we face? And how do we deal with them?

Here are five examples:

> ➢ Buyer claims others don't see any difference in your product / service, in relation to others they could buy.

Always conduct sales meetings with decision makers and people who influence them.

➢ Buyer leads you to believe you can do business with them if you offer a lower price.

Stick to you price as customers speak to each other.

➢ Buyer tries to force a fixed unit price on you.

Never itemise how you build your price. If you have set packages then only talk in terms of a package price. Do not be coerced into lowering your price.

➢ Buyer says 'use our name as a reference.'

You can use their name anyway and it's not a reason to reduce your price.

➢ Buyer insists they need a prototype.

State that you'll charge for it because it's an expensive undertaking. However, if they go on-to buy from you then the cost can be applied to the purchase price.

How can we improve our selling technique?

The focus of selling has changed significantly from promoting the features of a product or service to helping buyers achieve their objectives. As a result of this a lot more is required from your sales team. In terms of approach they should have a combination of problem-solving skills and act as a personal concierge to beneficiaries, customers and clients.

Consumer expectations have changed and one of the reasons for this is because the internet has given them a tool to research products and services. Also, they can compare and contrast in a variety of different ways and with ease. Therefore, they engage with your organisation beyond your offering, they are looking for a positive experience.

You can achieve this by offering a personal service. This is where you relieve potential buyers of any queries, concerns and enable a truly seamless interaction. Wherever possible, provide demonstrations of your product or service. In his book, **The Apprentice – How to Get Hired Not Fired, Lord Alan Sugar** offers this **practical tip.**

"If you are selling your services or promoting a product, your clients want to be able to believe in what you're offering them. Make sure you come across as a safe bet. If you have a problem with self-confidence, hide your fear. Feeling nervous and uncertain in new situations is normal. You'll soon adapt."

Train your sales team to think and behave like a project manager for each buyer. Also, ensure they are fully aware of marketing and promotion methods used to attract buyers. Try to prevent a disconnection between all of these functions.

Selling via social media

The advent of developed peer to peer advice, referrals and insights has taken over traditional marketing brochures. As a consequence of this, cultivating relationships on social networks is increasingly becoming the way forward to selling your offerings.

From a sales perspective, social media is most effective at the lead generation, exploring opportunities and research stage, prior to meeting prospects, face to face. Indicators that suggest you may have potential customers are: discussions on online forums, complaints on Facebook, or questions posted on Twitter. If they resonate with the solution you are offering they are warm leads. Your response to their query is the beginning of a dialogue which could lead to a sales meeting.

Use Hootesuite to help you identify potential social leads, with needs. It is a monitoring tool that acts like as radar to identify needs. If you want to use LinkedIn to build a prospects network, send invitations to connect with people. Then follow up with an email, tweet or phone call. The social profile of your sales representative should leave readers with the impression that they skilled and knowledgeable.

Managing online relationships

Firstly, make a point of finding out as much as you can about your customer. Engage with them about issues that are meaningful to them. Remember that sales, is about a relationship focused activity.

Secondly, choose one day a week which will be assigned to writing a blog post that specifically addresses an issue, need or concern of your target audience. Other trustees and staff can tweet, offer 'likes' on Facebook and share an update on LinkedIn. Your customers may choose to follow your representative and may go onto retweet the blog post. This in turn enhances your viral marketing activity and furthers brand awareness and equity.

We want to write a direct mail sales letter, what can we do to better understand our niche audience?

Understanding the psyche and motivations of your audience are crucial in all sales situations but even more so in a sales letter. The reason for this is because in a sales letter you cannot see or feel the reactions of the reader. Nor can you immediately respond to their queries, questions or concerns.

Therefore, everything you convey in your letter really does need to stimulate their emotions and lead them along the path to saying yes to your call to action. Here are four actions you can take to gain an appreciation of your intended audience:

> ➤ Participate in regular mastermind groups and meetings with people who deliver services to your market.

> ➤ Read all relevant industry magazines and blogs, every month.

> ➤ Follow and contribute to discussion forums, tailored to your audience.

> ➤ Attend seminars, conferences and events related to your sector.

When you've digested all the relevant information and you're ready to write your sales letter, composing a good headline will attract people to read your letter. Headlines are great statements that are expressed positively or negatively that engage people on how they either:

> ➤ Save, acquire or achieve something by using your product or service.

> ➤ Avoid, decrease or remove risks, mistakes, or embarrassment through using your product or service.

Examples of these types of headlines are:

To people who want to get fit but can't get started.

In this instance the target audience is very clear and they want to achieve something. However, they have difficulty in moving forward. Conversely,

How much is workplace stress costing your organisation?

Here, the reader may be curious about knowing more examples of workplace stress. How much is it costing their organisation? And they may want to know what they can do about it.

Buyers' motivation

People are encouraged to buy things when these types of sales tactics are incorporated in the sales process:

> ➤ Stating that a limited number of what you're offering is available. And, if they respond after this number has been exhausted, then they can no longer take advantage of your offer.

> ➤ Adding a strong guarantee and if someone is dissatisfied with their purchase, you will refund their money.

> ➤ Highlighting a great story about how your product or service has helped others improve their lives.

Selling skills…We might even impress Lord Alan Sugar!

Mini workout

1. Over the next 3 months list practices you are going to develop to build rapport with your users.

2. Write a 2 page statement highlighting how you will manage a complex monitoring process.

3. Design your organisational story clearly identifying the attributes you will use to sell it to your audience.

4. Identify your worst performing service and structure a pitch that you will use to sell the improvements to your beneficiaries.

5. Write a sales headline that will help your users acquire something.

Afterword

I hope that you enjoyed reading Non-Profit Booster and that it has helped to refresh your thinking and approaches on leading your organisation towards success.

Remember your journey towards making the world a better place requires:

- Clear leadership that guides the organisation's strategy.

- A unified team who are committed to the strategy.

- Creating an internal environment that speaks positively to everyone who comes into contact with the organisation.

- Understanding and communicating the value proposition that helps to structure the business model.

- Relating to your beneficiaries and stakeholders to the extent that they want to become advocates for your brand.

- Selecting the collaborators and partners who compliment what your organisation represents and adds value to your beneficiaries.

- Developing the organisation's intellectual property to create physical and digital products and services.

- Knowing how to develop marketing and promotional messages that lead to the sales of your mission, products or services.

- Harnessing the power of social media and digital tools to continue to transmit your online communications.

As you rise up to meet the spirit and intentions of your vision and mission statements, take Non-Profit Booster along as a constant companion.

"The future belongs to those who believe in the beauty of their dreams."

Eleanor Roosevelt (1884–1962), First Lady, Social Activist, Author, Lecturer and U.S. Representative to the United Nations

Glossary

Donor: An individual, company or organisation that makes a pledge, grant or contribution to a non-profit organisation.

Grant: Usually a cash award from a funder to an eligible organisation, for a specific purpose.

Leverage: This is a process that enables individuals or organisations to use relationships, assets or money to create a better advantage.

Marketing: The process of raising awareness of your service, brand or product to potential customers and the wider public, with the intention of generating sales.

Mission statement: This is a clear description that reflects what an organisation does, for whom, the geographic area the service is delivered in and the benefits that beneficiaries will gain, by using the service.

Non-profit organisation: An entity that delivers services, products and programmes to service users, without making a profit and receives funding and other resources from donors who do not expect a similar return in value.

Partnership: A structure that allows for a contractual arrangement that enables two or more organisations to work together.

Stakeholder: Anyone who has an interest in the work of the organisation.

Strategic plan: A document that summarises board decisions about how the organization aims to deliver its outcomes, over a specific period in time.

S.W.O.T: Relates to the strengths, weaknesses, opportunities and threats that organisations give consideration when undertaking an internal planning process.

Trustees: Voluntary leadership team that implements the legal role of governance for non-profit organisations:

Vision: An internally shared image of the type of impact the organisation will achieve in the future.

Appendix 1

10 top tips to build your annual report

1. **Highlight your accomplishments, not your activities**

   Your audiences are keen to know what you actually achieved during the year. As opposed to giving them a routine list of your services. People are keen to understand the rationale for why you delivered what you did. In addition, they want to know the outcomes that were achieved. And what difference you made.

   Demonstrate clearly how the daily activities flow directly from your mission statement. This will help your audience to understand your organisational strategy.

2. **Don't overload the annual report with operational minutiae**

   Avoid including: installing a wireless internet connection, or improved staff efficiencies because they each work from their own iPad. The reason for non-inclusion is because these factors do not relate directly to the mission statement. You can discuss operational issues at board and staff meetings.

3. **Don't focus too heavily on fundraising achievements**

   You are in the business of delivering services, so your stakeholders expect you to raise money and acquire resources to do so. They will be far more interested in what the money was spent on as opposed to knowing who was involved and how was it raised. If you want to reflect on fundraising successes, include it in the financial section of the annual report.

4. **Annual reports are also visual mediums**

   So tell your organisation's story by including photos these can be ones you've actually taken of actual events, services or products. Alternatively, if you don't have any, you can buy public domain photos. You can search the internet for 'royalty free photographs'.

5. **Add words to your photographs**

   Write a punchy statement against each photo that connects it to an achievement. Throughout the annual report you want to be demonstrating

Non-Profit Booster | 159

the powerful and positive impact your organisation is having.

6. Write profiles of real people

Funders, donors and investors will be more engaged and impressed if you include information about real people. You should humanise the facts and figures in the annual report. You can do this by showing how your service has practically helped specific beneficiaries. Or include an example of how a volunteer has contributed to the service and how volunteering has helped to improve their life.

7. Clarify the financial position of the organisation

Some of your stakeholders may not know how to read a financial statement. Therefore, this is a good opportunity for you to explain things to them. You could touch on the components of your income generating strategy.

8. Acknowledge contributors and donors

Thank you, are two powerful words that donors and contributors will be very pleased to hear from you. Don't forget to include them. If you have a long list of names, think of other ways that you could publicly acknowledge them. This is particularly so if the list of names could take up 50% or more of the annual report. If this is the case, maybe you can include them on your website, blog or newsletter.

9. **Spell everyone's name properly**

If in doubt about the correct spelling of a name, double check it with the person concerned, as you don't want to cause offence.

10. **Solicit help from potential donors**

Your annual report is a P.R. and marketing tool. Therefore, be clear about how people can support you in the future. Hopefully, you have shown all the great value that your organisation has added to the lives of beneficiaries. If so, tell people how they can help you to do more.

Appendix 2

Donor evaluation form

Your name:
....

Category	Name and email	Why could this person be a major donor?	Date I will contact this person
My doctor			
My dentist			
My accountant			
My broker			
My banker			
My lawyer			

Donor evaluation form

Your name:

....

Category	Name and email	Why could this person be a major donor?	Date I will contact this person
Relatives			
Friends			

Donor evaluation form

Your name:

....

Category	Name and email	Why could this person be a major donor?	Date I will contact this person
Sports team			
Local or national politicians			

Donor evaluation form

Your name:

....

Category	Name and email	Why could this person be a major donor?	Date I will contact this person
Professional associations			
Social networks			

Donor evaluation form

Your name:

....

Category	Name & email	Why could this person be a major donor?	Date I will contact this person
Clients			
Business associates			

Donor evaluation form

Your name:

....

Category	Name & email	Why could this person be a major donor?	Date I will contact this person
Volunteers			
Others			

Appendix 3

Your 2 page business plan

Answer each question or statement with a couple of short sentences.

Moving forward

What are the organisation's objectives?

What will you sell?

Who is your customer or client?

How will your product or service help people?

Show me the money

How much will you charge?

What methods of payment will you offer?

What other ways could you generate income from your product or service?

Shine your light in the world

How will customers know about your organisation and what you are selling?

What will you do to encourage people to make referrals?

Reaching your target

What indicators will you use to determine success?

Problems

Identify a problem you may face on your journey to success.

How will you overcome it?

Appendix 4

General Resources

Action steps to be taken in the next 30 days

1.

2.

3.

4.

5.

6.

7.

8.

9.

10.

10 totally terrific books to add to your bookshelf

Gary Vaynerchuk, Crush It! Why Now is the Time To Cash In On Your Passion, Harper Studio, 2009

Brad Burton, Get Off Your Arse, 4 Publishing, 2009

Dr. Robert B Cialdini, Influence –The Psychology of Persuasion, HarperCollins, 2007

Ricardo Semler, Maverick, Random House, 1993

Blair Singer, Sales Dogs, Hachette Book Group, 2001

Sir Richard Branson, Screw It, Let's Do It Expanded, Virgin Books Limited, 2007

David Plouffe, The Audacity to Win – The Inside Story and Lessons Of Barack Obama's Historic Victory, Penguin Group, 2009

Stephen Denning, The Leader's Guide to Radical Management – Reinventing the Workplace for the 21st Century, John Wiley & Sons, 2010

Tony Dungy, The Mentor Leader – Secrets to Building People and Teams That Win Consistently, Tyndale House, 2010

Dr. David Lewis and Darren Bridger, The Soul of the New Consumer – Authenticity, What We Buy and Why in the New Economy, Nicholas Brealey Publishing, 2000

And others that maybe of interest

Sir John Whitmore, Coaching for Performance – Growing People, Performance and Purpose, Nicholas Brealey Publishing, 2003

Carayol and David Firth, Corporate Voodoo: Principle for Business Mavericks and Magicians, Capstone Publishing, Limited (A Wiley Company). 2001

Francis Horibe, Creating the Innovation Culture: Leveraging Visionaries, Dissenters and Other Useful Trouble-makers, John Wiley & Sons (Canada), 2001

Jim Collins, Good to Great, Random Press, 2001

Audit Commission, Governing Partnerships: Bridging the Accountability Gap, 2005

Dale Carnegie, How to Win Friends and Influence People, Vermillion, 1998

Jake Steinfeld, I've Seen a Lot of Famous People Naked and They've Got Nothing on You: Business Secrets From The Ultimate Street-Smart Entrepreneur, Amacom, 2006

R.A. Heifetz, Leadership without Easy Answers, Belnap Press, 1994

Lord Alan Sugar, The Apprentice – How to Get Hired Not Fired, BBC Books, 2005

Geoff Mulgan, The Art of Public Policy: Mobilising Power and Knowledge for the Common Good, Oxford University Press, 2009

Ricado Semler, The Seven Day Weekend: A Better Way to Work in the 21st Century, Century, 2003

Stephen Covey, The 7 Habits of Highly Effective People: Powerful Lessons in Personal Change, Simon & Schuster UK, 2004

R.T. Hogan, G.J. Curphy and J. Hogan, What Do You Know About Leadership? American Psychologist, 49 (1994), 493-504

Some useful organisations

United Kingdom

Association of Charitable Foundations
14 Upper Woburn Place, London, WC1H OAE
Tel: 0207 255 4499, Email: acf@acf.org.uk
Website: www.ac.org.uk

Business in the Community
England
137 Shepherdess Walk, London, N1 7RQ
Tel: 0207 566 8650, Email: information@bitc.org.uk

Scotland
Livingstone House, 1st Floor, 43a Discovery Terrace,
Heriot-Watt Research Park, Edinburgh, EH14 4AP
Tel: 0131 451 1100, Email: info@sbcscot.com

Wales
Cardiff Office, 2nd Floor, Riverside House,
31 Cathedral Road, Cardiff, CF11 9HB
Tel: 029 2078 0050, Email: information@bitc.org.uk

Mold Office, St. Andrews Park, Queens Lane, Mold,
CH7 1XB
Tel: 01352 706213, Email: wales@bitc.org.uk

Website: www.bitc.org.uk

Charities Aid Foundation
25 Kings Hill Avenue, Kings Hill, West Malling, Kent,
ME19 4TA
Tel: 03000 123 000,
Website: www.cafonline.org

Charity Commission (England and Wales)
PO Box 1227, Liverpool, L69 3UG
Tel: 0845 3000 218,
Email: admin@charitycommission.gov.uk
Website:www.charitycommission.gov.uk

Charity Commission for Northern Ireland
257 Lough Road, Lurgan, Craigavon, BT66 6NQ
Tel: 028 3832 0220,
Email: admin@charitycommissionni.org.uk
Website: www.charitycommissionni.org.uk

Charities Evaluation Service
4 Coldbath Square, London, ECIR 5HL
Tel: 0207 713 5722, Email: enquiries@ces-vol.org.uk
Website: www.ces-vol.org.uk

Charity Trends
Tel: 03000 123 111
Website: www.charitytrends.org

Companies House
Crown Way, Cardiff, CF4 3UZ
Tel: 01222 380801
Website: www.companieshouse.gov.uk

Directory of Social Change
London Office
24 Stephenson Way, London, NW1 2DP
Tel: 0207 391 4800, Email: training@dsc.org.uk

Liverpool Office
Federation House, Hope Street, Liverpool, L1 9BW
Tel: 0151 708 0117, Email: research@dsc.org.uk

Website: www.dsc.org.uk

Fit4Funding (The Charities Information Bureau)
Lightwaves, Lower York Street, Wakefield, WF1 3LJ
Telephone: 01924 239063,
Email: info@fit4funding.org.uk
Website: www.fit4funding.org.uk

Institute of Fundraising
Park Place, 12 Lawn Lane, London, SW8 1UD
Tel: 0207 840 1000,
Email: enquiries@institute-of-fundraising.org.uk
Website: www.institute-of-fundraising.org.uk

Media Trust
4th Floor, Block A, Centre House, London W12 7SB
Tel: 0207 871 5600, Email: info@mediatrust.org
Website: www.mediatrust.org

National Association of Voluntary and Community
Action
The Tower, 2 Furnival Square, Sheffield, S1 4QL
Tel: 0114 2786636, Email: navca@navca.org.uk
Website: www.navca.org.uk

National Council for Voluntary Organisations
Regent's Wharf, 8 All Saints Street, London, N1 9RL
Tel: 0207 713 6161, Email: ncvo@ncvo-vol.org.uk
Website: www.ncvo-vol.org.uk

New Economics Foundation
3 Jonathan Street, London SE11 5NH
Tel: 020 7820 6300, Email: info@neweconomics.org
www.neweconomics.org

Northern Ireland Council for Voluntary Action
61 Duncairn Gardens, Belfast, BT15 2GB
Tel: 028 9087 777, Email: info@nicva.org
Website: www.nicva.org

Office of the Scottish Charity Regulator
2nd Floor, Quadrant House, 9 Riverside Drive, Dundee, DD1 4NY
Tel: 01382 220446, Email: info@oscr.org.uk
Website: www.oscr.org.uk

Office for Civil Society
2nd Floor, Admiralty Arch, South Side, The Mall, London SW1A 2WH
Tel: 0207 819 1200, Email: info@civilsociety.co.uk
Website:www.civilsociety.co.uk

Resource Alliance
Head Office, 5th Floor Development House
56-64 Leonard Street, London, EC2A 4LT
Tel: 0207 065 0810,
Email: contact@resource-alliance.org
Website: www.resource-alliance.org

Scottish Council for Voluntary Organisations
Mansfield Traquair Centre, 15 Mansfield Place, Edinburgh EH3 6BB
Tel: 0131 474 8000, Email: enquiries@scvo.org.uk
Website: www.scvo.org.uk

Skoll Centre for Social Entrepreneurship
Said Business School, University of Oxford, Park End Street, Oxford, OX1 1HP
Tel: 01865 288838, Email skollcentre@sbs.ox.ac.uk
Website: www.sbs.ox.ac.uk/skoll

Small Charities Coalition
24 Stephenson Way, London, NW1 2DP
Tel: 0207 391 4812, Email: info@smallcharities.org.uk
Website: www.smallcharities.org.uk

Social Enterprise UK
The Fire Station, 139 Tooley Street, London, SE1 2HZ
Tel: 0203 589 4950,
Email: info@socialenterprise.org.uk
Website: www.socialenterprise.org.uk

The Funding Network
16 Lincoln's Inn Fields, London, WC2A 3ED
Tel: 0845 313 8449,
Email: info@thefundingnetwork.org.uk
Website: www.thefundingnetwork.org.

Volunteering England
Regent's Wharf, 8 All Saints Street, London, N1 9RL
Tel: 0207 520 8900, Email: ncvo@ncvo.org.uk
Website: www.volunteering.org.uk

Wales Council for Voluntary Action
Baltic House, Mount Stuart Square, Cardiff Bay,
Cardiff, CF10 5FH
Tel: 0800 2888 329,
Email: enquiries@wcva.org.uk/volunteering
Website: www.volunteering.org.uk

International organisations
Africa

African Women's Development Fund
The African Women's Development Fund (AWDF) is a grant making foundation that supports local, national and regional women's organisations working towards the empowerment of African women and the promotion and realisation of their rights.

PMB CT, 89 Cantonments, Accra, Ghana
Tel: 233 (0) 302 521257 / 233 289 669666,
Email: grants@awdf.org Website: awdf@awdf.org

STAR Foundation
Delivers Impact Awards and Impact Partnerships to help effective charities become even stronger.

11 Belgrave Road, London, SW1V 1RB
Tel: 0870 334 9000,
Email: info@starsfoundation.org.uk :
Website: www.starsfoundation.org.uk

America

Ashoka Innovators for the Public (Operates Internationally)
Supports social entrepreneurs who are leading and collaborating with change-makers. They believe that anyone can learn and apply the critical skills of empathy, team work, leadership and change-making to be successful in the modern world.

Global Headquarters, 1700 North Moore Street, Suite 2000 (20th Floor), Arlington, VA 22209
Tel: 703-527-8300, Email: info@ashoka.org
Website: www.ashoka.org

Association of Fundraising Professionals
A professional association of individuals and organisations that generate philanthropic support across the world, for a range of institutions.

4300 Wilson Blvd, Suite 300, Arlington, Virginia 22203
Tel: 703 684 0410, Email: afp@afpnet.org
Website: www.afpnet.org

Association of Small Foundations
A membership organisation for donors, trustees, employees and consultants of foundations that have few or no staff.

1720 N Street, NW, Washington, DC 20036
Tel: 202 580-6560, Email: asf@smallfoundations.org
Website: www.smallfoundations.org

Community Wealth Ventures
Helps change agents solve social problems in their local communities.

1730 M Street, NW Suite 700, Washington, DC 20036
Tel: 202 478 6570, Email: info@communitywealth.com
Website: www.communitywealth.com

Central New York Community Foundation
Encourages local philanthropy by supporting the growth of a permanent charitable endowment to improve the region.

431 East Fayette Street, Suite 100, Syracuse, NY 13202
Tel: 315 422 9538, Email: info@cnycf.org
Website: www.cnycf.org

Council on Foundations
Provides opportunities, leadership and tools for philanthropic organisations to expand, enhance and sustain their ability to advance the common good.

2121 Crystal Drive, Suite 700, Arlington, Virginia 22202
Tel: 800 673 9036, Email: membership@cof.org
Website: www.cof.org

The National Council of Non Profit Associations
Builds the capacity of local community organisations.
1200 New York Avenue NW, Suite 700, Washington, DC 20005
Tel: (202) 962-0322, Email: ncna@ncna.org
Website: www.ncna.org

The Philanthropic Initiative
An advisory team that designs and evaluates philanthropic programs for individual donors, families, foundations, and corporations.

420 Boylston Street, Boston, MA 02116
Tel: 617.338.2590, Email: get2us@tpi.org
Website: www.tpi.org

The Small Business Administration
Provides information on community development grant
programmes.

409 3rd Street, SW Washington DC 20416
Tel: 202 205 6510, Email: answerdesk@sba.gov
Website: www.sba.gov/INV

The United Way (USA and Internationally)
Improves lives by mobilising the power of communities
around the world to advance the common good.

Website: www.unitedway.org

WANGO
Helps to provide the mechanism and support needed
for N.G.Os to connect, partner, share, inspire, and mul-
tiply their contributions to solve humanity's basic
problems.

WANGO International Headquarters 200 White Plains
Road, First Floor, Tarrytown, NY 10591, USA
Email: secretariat@wango.org

WANGO Africa Regional Secretariat
2nd floor Gidan Abbas MG, 12 Sultan Road GRA, PO
Box 9689 Kaduna 800001 Nigeria
Email: africa@wango.org

Office of United Nations Affairs
866 United Nations Plaza, Suite 529
New York, NY 10017, USA
Email: unoffice@wango.org
Website: www.wango.org

Australia

The Funding Network
Raises funds for innovative social change projects
through collaborative giving.

Level 4, 15-17 Young Street
Sydney, NSW 2000
Website: www.thefundingnetwork.com.au

Sydney Community Foundation
Funds worthy projects and allows donors to fulfil their
charitable goals both during and after their lifetime.

PO Box R454, Royal Exchange NSW 1225
Tel: 02 9251 1228
Email: enquiries@sydneycommunityfoundation.org.au
Web: www.sydneycommunityfoundation.org.au

Belgium

Solidar
European network of NGOs working to advance social
justice in Europe and worldwide.

Rue du Commerce 22, 1000 Brussels
Tel: +32 (0)2 500 10 20 Email:
Website: www.solidar.org

European Venture Philanthropy Association
A membership association made up of organisations

interested in or practicing venture philanthropy and social investment across Europe.

78 Avenue de la Toison d'Or, 1060 Brussels, Belgium
Tel: +32 (0) 2.513.21.31, Email: info@evpa.eu.com
Website: www.evpaeu.com

Caribbean

The Caribbean N.G.O. Database.
Contains details of organisations across the Caribbean. It is owned by the N.G.O. Caribbean Development Foundation.

141 Duke Street, Port of Spain, Trinidad, West Indies.
Tel: 868-792-2089, Email: contact@ngocaribbean.org
Website: www.ngocaribbean.org

China

China Development Brief
The publication contains a range of articles on: NGO development and capacity building, volunteerism, philanthropy, civic participation, independent research and media.

15 Zhonggu Hutong, Songzhuyuan Beixiang, Beiheyan Dajie, Dongcheng Qu, Beijing 100009, PRC
Tel: 86 (0)10-6407 1400/8402 5759/8402 2532
Email: inquiries@chinadevelopmentbrief.cn
Website: www.chinadevelopmentbrief.cn

Europe

Volonteurope Secretariat CSV
An international network promoting the values and principles of volunteering, active citizenship and social justice at local, regional, national and European levels.

237 Pentonville Road, London, N1 9NJ
Tel: 0207 643 1329, Email: info@volonteurope.eu
Website: www.volonteurope.eu

France

Itineraire International
Promotes international mobility for young adults between 18 to 30 years old, whatever qualifications they have.

Tel: 0033966921765
E-mail: clementine.laforet@itineraire-international.org
Website: http://www.itineraire-international

Germany

Academy of Volunteering Germany (Akademie fur Ehrenamtlichkeit Deutschland)
A training and consulting institution especially for Volunteering, citizen engagement and honorary posts.

Email: Andy Fryar at andy@ozvpm.com
Website: www.volunteermanagersday.org

India

NGOs India
An online web directory and resource centre for organisations based in India.

Chanakya, 302, Riddhi Siddhi Complex, Madhuban,
Udaipur 313001, Rajasthan, India
Tel: Mobile: +91 9309243040,
Email: info@ngosindia.com
Website: www.ngosindia.com

Latin America

Casa Alianza
An international, non-governmental organisation
dedicated to the rehabilitation and defence of street
children in Honduras, Nicaragua, Mexico and
Guatemala. The organisation also has European
offices in the U.K. Germany and Switzerland.

Unit 2, The Business Exchange, Rockingham Road,
Kettering, Northants, NN16 8J X
Tel: 01536 526 447, Email: casalnzauk@gn.apc.org
Website: www.casa-alianza.org

New Zealand

The Trusts Community Foundation
Distributes funds generated from Class 4 gaming
machines operated in some licensing trusts outlets,
privately owned hotels and a bowling club throughout
New Zealand.

TTCF, Private Bag 93108, Henderson, Auckland 0650
Tel: 0800 882 3583, Email: grants@ttcfltd.org.nz
Website: www.ttcfltd.org.nz

Russia

Moscow Youth Multifunctional Center
A youth focused organisation established by the
Moscow Government. The aim is to inspire and involve

active young people in projects based around; business innovations and international projects.

Tel: +7 (499) 181 83 64, Email: info@mymfc.ru
Website: www.mymfc.ru

Useful websites

Banks

Charity Bank
www.charitybank.org

The Co-operative Bank
www.co-operativebank.co.uk

The Ecology Building Society
www.ecology.co.uk

Royal Bank of Scotland
www.rbs.co.uk

Triodos Bank
www.triodos.co.uk

Unity Trust Bank
www.unity.uk.com

Other financiers

Baring English Growth Fund
www.begf.co.uk

Bridges Community Ventures
www.bridgesventures.com

Catalyst Social Fund
www.catfund.com

Charities Aid Foundation and Venturesome
www.cafonline.org

Coalfields Enterprise Fund
www.englishpartnerships.co.uk

Community Development Finance Institutions
www.cdfa.org.uk

Foursome Investments Limited
www.foursome.net

Industrial Common Ownership Finance
www.icof.co.uk

Local Investment Fund
www.lif.org.uk

The Prince's Trust
www.princes-trust.org.uk

Regional Venture Capital Funds
www.sbs.gov.uk

Foundations

Lloyds TSB Foundation
www.lloydstsbfoundations.org.uk

The Baring Foundation
www.baringfoundation.org.uk

The Elton John Foundation
www.ejaf.org

The Gatsby Foundation
www.gatsby.org.uk

The Gulbenkian Foundation
www.gulbenkian.org.uk

UK Community Foundations
www.ukcommunityfoundations.org

Funding portals

Community Foundation Network
www.communityfoundations.org.uk

Company Giving
www.companygiving.org.uk

Government Funding
www.governmentfunding.org.uk

GRANTfinder
www.grantfinder.co.uk

Grants for Individuals
www.grantsforindividuals.org.uk

Grants Online
www.grantsonline.org.uk

Trust Funding
www.trustfunding.org.uk

Technology and digital resources

Base Camper
Project management tool
www.basecamper.com

Blog Talk Radio
Social radio network
www.blogtalkradio.com

Crowding In
Crowd funding directory
www.crowdingin.com

Drop Box
File sharing portal
www.dropbox.com

Elance
Freelancer job site
www.elance.com

Ezine Articles
Expert knowledge platform
www.ezinearticles.com

Freedom
Productivity app
www.macfreedom.com

Freelancer
Freelancer jobs site
www.freelancer.com

Friendfeed
Online sharing content site
www.friendfeed.com

Go to Meeting
Online meeting facility
www.gotomeeting.com

Go Daddy
Domain name registrar
www.godaddy.com

Go to Webinar
Online training facility
www.gotowebinar.com

Google for Non-Profits
Resources to help with donor engagement
www.google.com/nonprofits

Help a Reporter
Experts and reporters portal
www.helpareporter.com

Instagram
Photo and video sharing tool
www.instagram.com

Odesk
Freelancer job site
www.odesk.com

Pinterest
Visual theme platform
www.pinterest.com

Roboform
Password manager
www.roboform.com

Slideshare
Presentation portal
www.slideshare.com

Survey Monkey
Survey software
www.surveymonkey.com

Tech Crunch
Technology media site
www.techcrunch.com

Tinychat
Video chat platform
www.tinychat.com

Tumblr
Blogging platform
www.tumblr.com

Ustream
Live video broadcast site
www.ustream.com

Viddler
Online video facility
www.viddler.com

Resources from Insights to Impact

Join a free 1 hour webinar

Now that you have read Non Profit Booster, join the author Bybreen Samuels on a live webinar. Here's your chance to expand upon themes from the book at a deeper level. Also, you'll have the chance to have some of your burning questions, answered.

To register for the webinar, send an email to: feelinggood@.nonprofitbooster.com Write, **free 1 hour webinar** in the subject line.

Audio version of Non-Profit Booster

Turn your car or home into a university by buying a copy of and listening to the audio version of Non-Profit Booster.

To register your interest for this product, send an email to: feelinggood@nonprofitbooster.com Write, **'Audio Version'** in the subject line. Or use the **Quick Order Form** at the back of this book.

Organisational book booster seminar

Bybreen Samuels and Insights to Impact Publishing invite you and one other person to attend the Organisational Book Booster Seminar. At this two day event you will learn how to build and write your unique an appealing book about your organisation's story, benefits and achievements. Also, discover how this one product can lead to multiple streams of unrestricted income.

And you will gain knowledge about the publishing options that are available. Finally, you will find out tactics to market and promote your book.

To register your interest and to find out more information about costs and dates, send an email to: <u>feelinggood@nonprofitbooster.com</u> .

Write, **'organisational book booster seminar'** in the subject line. Or use the **Quick Order Form** at the back of this book.

Book buying options

Buy 10 books

I will create a 10 minute video teaching you how to craft an effective elevator pitch for your organisation. Email your receipt of purchase to: wow@nonprofitbooster.com **stating elevator pitch.**

Buy 25 books

Have a 20 minute conference call with me to discuss your issues or questions about your organisation. Email your receipt of purchase to: wow@nonprofitbooster.com **stating conference call.**

Buy 50 books

I will deliver an introductory governance assessment for your organisation. Email your receipt of purchase to wow@nonprofitbooster.com **stating governance audit.**

Buy 100 books

I will deliver a one hour practical workshop webinar. Email your receipt of purchase to: wow@nonprofitbooster.com **stating webinar.**

Buy 250 books

I will deliver a 90 minute in person seminar, in the U.K. And you can enjoy the office gourmet and goodie hamper that you will also receive. Email your receipt of purchase to wow@nonprofitbooster.com **stating 90 minute in person seminar.**

Buy 500 books

You will receive a one hour audit of an aspect of your organisation. Also, you'll get 3 special gifts that can be given to members of staff and / or volunteers, who you consider to be organisational 'rock stars'. Email your receipt of purchase to wow@nonprofitbooster.com **stating 1 hour audit.**

Buy 1000 books

I will deliver a one hour keynote speech including a Q & A, in the U.K. The keynote will be followed by a book signing session. Plus you'll receive ten special gifts to be given to your choice of service users and staff. Email your receipt of purchase to:
wow@nonprofitbooster.com **stating keynote speech.**

If you would like me to deliver this opportunity outside the U.K. send an email to bybreen@nonprofitbooster.com **to discuss your offer.**

An alternative option is you can make me an offer

If you want a variation on the book buying options, then I'm happy to receive reasonable alternative offers. Send me an email at: bybreen@nonprofitbooster.com stating your name, email, telephone number and how many books you're going to buy. Then indicate what your offer is in terms of what you want from me, in exchange.

Share your stories

After implementing the strategies and tactics in Non-Profit Booster, I would love to hear your experiences, stories, questions, ideas and solutions.

Also, if you would like to write a review of Non-Profit Booster, I welcome your contribution.

Send all comments to stories@nonprofitbooster.com

Index

Notes

Notes

ABOUT THE AUTHOR

Bybreen Samuels is an author, writer, speaker, teacher, coach and publisher. She helps non-profit organisations to develop and maximise their potential to delight their beneficiaries and other stakeholders.

Bybreen has extensive experience of working in and around non-profit organisations, since the 1990s. Her expertise incorporates assisting organisations to cultivate their ideas, through to raising money to implement them which leads to positive experiences for beneficiaries. A major success that she achieved was to raise £895,775, in one application, from The Big Lottery Fund, for a charity partnership, in London.

Bybreen says, "Too many organisations struggle with their development. I know that I can definitely help them identify what their barriers to success are. And then I provide them with strategies, tactics and tools to overcome their challenges."

Bybreen is a Winston Churchill Fellow. This leadership award led her to China, where she undertook a research project to explore employment and lifestyle practices for older people. She rates this whole experience as 'outstanding'. She also, has an L.L.B. Honours Degree in Law and an MSc in the Psychodynamics of Human Development

Whatever your development challenge

......There is a solution!

Call Bybreen on: 0208 761 2003

Skype her at: Skype ID: bybreen

Email her at: bybreen@nonprofitbooster.com

Find out more at: www.nonprofitbooster.com

Connect with and follow her at:

Twitter @Bybreensamuels
www.medium.com/bybreensamuels
www.bybreen.tumblr.com
www.youtube.com/bybreen

Insights
to Impact

Insights to Impact Publishing

Quick order form

Email orders: wow@nonprofitbooster.com

Telephone / Skype orders: Call 0208 761 2003. Skype Identity: bybreen. Have your credit card ready.

Make cheques payable to Insights to Impact Limited.
Please send _____copy/copies of Non-Profit Booster (paperback and/or audio version.)

Please send more FREE information on other products – audio books, DVD course, speaking engagements, seminars and group coaching.

Name:_____

Address:_____

_____

City: _____**Country:**_____

Tel:_____

Email:_____

U.K. postage: Add an additional £2.60 per book / product posted in the U.K. **International postage:** Add an additional £6.00 for the first book / product and £4.50 for each additional book / product (estimate).

Payment: Paypal, cash, bank transfer, cheque or credit card:
Card number:

_____

Name on card:

_____

Expiry date:

_____